AN ADAPTED CLASSIC

The Jungle

Upton Sinclair

GLOBE FEARON EDUCATIONAL PUBLISHER
Upper Saddle River, New Jersey
www.globefearon.com

Adapter: Sandra Widener
Project Editor: Wendy R. Diskin
Senior Editor: Lynn Kloss
Production Editor: Travis Bailey
Marketing Manager: Gloria Sammur
Art Supervision: Sharon Ferguson
Electronic Page Production: Phyllis Rosinsky
Illustrator and Cover Illustration: Laurie Harden

Printed in the United States of America.
1 2 3 4 5 6 7 8 9 10 03 02 01 00 99

ISBN 0-835-94982-6

GLOBE FEARON EDUCATIONAL PUBLISHER
Upper Saddle River, New Jersey
www.globefearon.com

CONTENTS

ABOUT THE AUTHOR

Upton Sinclair is among the most widely known and celebrated modern American propagandist novelists. He devoted his life to battling social injustice. In his long lifetime (1878–1968) he remained true to the ideals that prompted him to write his most famous book, *The Jungle.*

Upton Sinclair was born in Baltimore to a poor family. When he was ten, the family moved to New York City. At the age of 14, he entered City College of New York. While there, he made money by writing novels about adventure. He went on to graduate school at Columbia University, but he left before receiving his degree.

In 1904, Sinclair discovered Socialism. Socialism is a social system in which the workers possess a political power and the means of producing and distributing goods. He became a believer. That same year, he was hired by the Socialist weekly newspaper, *The Appeal to Reason*, to look into the situation of workers at the Chicago stockyards. He spent seven weeks there, documenting what became a well-known series in *The Appeal to Reason.*

When the collected chapters were published as *The Jungle* in 1906, it was the first novel to make much money for Sinclair. The public was horrified by the terrible working conditions that Sinclair described in *The Jungle.* The government looked into Sinclair's findings. In spite of pressure from owners of the stockyards, Congress passed the Pure Food and Drug Act of 1906.

In 1932, Sinclair was nominated for the Nobel Prize. In the 1940s and 1950s, he wrote a series of 11 novels about a fictional character named Lanny Budd, a rich

American secret agent. One of these novels, *Dragon's Teeth*, published in 1942, focused on Germany under the Nazis. It won the 1943 Pulitzer Prize for fiction.

Throughout his writing career, Sinclair never forgot the politics that mattered so much to him. In 1920 he helped start the American Civil Liberties Union, which was founded to champion the rights of Americans.

Upton Sinclair died at the age of 90, in 1968. His legacy—a deep-rooted belief in the possibility of change—lives on. "You don't have to be satisfied with America as you find it," he wrote in 1962. "You can change it."

ADAPTER'S NOTE

In preparing this edition of *The Jungle*, we have kept as close as possible to Upton Sinclair's original words and style. We have changed some of the vocabulary. We have also shortened some chapters. Some of the footnotes explain difficult words. Other footnotes fill in historical details of the story.

PREFACE

Since it was written, *The Jungle* has been known as a book with a message. Sinclair was often quoted as saying that when he wrote the book, he aimed for the heart and by accident hit the stomach. In spite of the public reaction to descriptions of the meat that was being sold, Sinclair always regarded the oppression of the workers as his main message. The novel takes a powerful look at the bleak but compelling world of Chicago stockyard workers at the turn of the century. These workers were largely immigrants who had come to America to make their fortunes. In *The Jungle*, most of the main characters are immigrants from Lithuania. Once in Packingtown (Sinclair's name for the stockyards), the immigrants encountered almost every evil that could be found in American industry, politics, and society at the time. Unable to speak English, the immigrants were easily taken advantage of by those in power—the packers and their foremen, the police, the political bosses, and the real-estate dealers. Sinclair's realistic details of the worker and the desperate world of the stockyards aroused the interest of consumers and working people alike.

HISTORICAL BACKGROUND

The Jungle was published at a time when America had just seen the making of vast industrial fortunes. Government leaders listened to the concerns of business and believed that what was good for business was good for the country.

Upton Sinclair's activism was a reaction to this way of looking at the world. He was a part of a group of journalists and reformers who came to be called "muckrakers." This group challenged the abuses of industrial giants, such as the meatpacking industry. *The Jungle* is considered one of the most important muckraking efforts of its time. The major reason for the success of the book was Sinclair's research. He spent time making sure he got every detail right. He did not want to be accused of making anything up.

The publisher of *The Jungle* and the U.S. government conducted separate inspections of the Chicago meatpacking industry and stockyards. The conclusion of both inspections was that Sinclair's findings that he reported in *The Jungle* were true and not exaggerations. The packing industry executives tried to deny the charges. But the people believed Sinclair's information, and as one packinghouse executive said, "The sale of meat and meat products has been more than cut in two." The debate between the packers and the government came to a close when both the Pure Food and Drug Act and the Beef Inspection Act were passed into laws—less than six months after the first appearance of the book version of Sinclair's *The Jungle*.

Most of those who read the book were horrified by the unhealthy conditions of the meatpacking industry. Sinclair, though, hoped to interest his readers not just in the origins of the food they ate but in the lives of the people who worked in the packinghouses. Sinclair describes the brutal lives of the Packingtown workers to give readers a revealing example of "wage slavery." "Wage slavery" is a condition under capitalism—or an economic system in which the means of production and distribution are privately or corporately owned—in which the workers think of themselves as free when, in fact, they are not. Rather, the workers are "slaves" to their bosses and the wages they pay them—however unfair.

Sinclair offered only one solution to the problems of the workers: Socialism. Socialism, as Sinclair and his fellow Socialists in America saw it then, would help workers come out from under the thumb of the industries that underpaid and mistreated them. Sinclair dreamed of a world in which the workers would own the packing companies. If that were true, Sinclair believed, wages, working conditions, and health practices would be better.

Sinclair's book, *The Jungle*, did not bring about a social revolution. Yet it played an important part in awakening people in the United States to the cruel and unjust treatment of workers by "big business."

MAJOR CHARACTERS

Jurgis Rudkus
Husband of Ona

Ona (Lukoszaite) Rudkus
Wife of Jurgis

Marija Berczynskas
Ona's cousin

Dede (Grandfather) Antanas Rudkus
Jurgis's father

Teta (Aunt) Elzbieta Lukoszaite
Ona's stepmother

Jonas
Elizbieta's brother, Ona's uncle

Tamoszius Kuszleika
Musician and Marija's boyfriend

Jokubas Szedvilas
Delicatessen owner and a friend of Jurgis

Grandmother Majauszkiene
Neighbor of Jurgis and his family

Jack Duane
Ex-convict and a friend of Jurgis

Freddie Jones
Rich stranger who takes Jurgis in

Ostrinski
Socialist reformer and friend of Jurgis

Stanislovas, Kotrina, Vilimas, and Nikalojus
Elzbieta's children

Chapter 1

It was four o'clock when the ceremony was over and the carriages began to arrive. The occasion rested heavily on Marija's shoulders—it was her task to see that all things followed the best traditions from their homeland. She had left the church last of all but wished to arrive first at the banquet hall. The music had started up, and half a block away you could hear the dull "broom, broom" of a cello. Marija sprang from her carriage and cleared a way to the banquet hall, which was the rear room of a saloon in a part of Chicago known as "back of the yards."

It was the hour of ecstasy for little Ona Lukoszaite, for it was the scene of her wedding feast. She stood in the door, guarded by Cousin Marija. There was a light of wonder in her eyes. She wore a white muslin dress and a stiff little veil. She was so young—not quite 16—and small for her age. She had just been married to Jurgis Rudkus, of all men, he with the mighty shoulders and the giant hands.

Ona was blue-eyed and fair, while Jurgis had great black eyes and thick black hair. Jurgis could pick up a 250-pound quarter of beef and carry it without a stagger. Now he stood in a far corner, frightened as a hunted animal.

If any onlooker came close or looked hungry, a chair was offered to him. It was one of the laws of the wedding feast that no one goes hungry. While a rule made in the forest of Lithuania is hard to apply in the stockyards of Chicago, with its quarter of a million inhabitants, still they did their best. The celebration was charmingly informal. The men wore their hats or took them off. Many of the older people wore clothing reminiscent[1] of home. This was carefully avoided by the young, who dressed in the latest styles. There were to be speeches, but no one had to listen. The resulting medley distracted no one, except possibly the babies. The older children marched about munching contentedly on bologna sausages.

There was a little person who led a musical trio. Tamoszius Kuszleika was his name, and he taught himself to play the violin after working all day on the "killing beds."[2] He was in his shirtsleeves, with a vest decorated with faded gold horseshoes, and a pink-striped shirt. He was only about five feet tall, but even so his trousers were about eight inches short of the ground. Now he was in his glory. Some of the people were eating, some were laughing, but every one of them heard him. This was their music, the music of home. The slums faded away, and there were sunlit rivers and mighty forests. Now and then one leapt up and gave a cry for this song or that, and away they went.

Little Ona was too excited to eat. Once in a while she ate, when Cousin Marija pinched her and reminded her, but mostly she sat gazing with the same fearful eyes of wonder. The music kept calling, and the far-off look came back, and she sat with her hands pressed over her heart. Then the tears came into her eyes, and she flushed red when she saw Jurgis watching her. When Tamoszius reached her side, Ona's cheeks were scarlet, and she looked as if she wanted to run away.

She was saved in this crisis by Marija. Marija wished to hear a song, and as the musicians did not

---

1. **reminiscent** reminding one
2. **killing beds** a room in the packing plants where cattle are slaughtered

know it, she was proceeding to teach them. Marija was short but powerful in build. She worked in a canning factory handling cans of beef that weighed 14 pounds. She had a broad face with red cheeks. As she roared her song, the musicians followed her.

It was time for a speech, and Dede[3] Antanas, Jurgis's father, rose. He was only 60, but you would have thought he was 80. His six months in America had not been good for him. In his manhood he had worked in a cotton mill, but then a hacking cough fell upon him. Out in the country the cough disappeared, but he had been working here in the pickle rooms at Durham's, and the cold damp air brought back his cough.

Dede Antanas had been a scholar in his youth, and he had composed a speech. Everyone drew near to listen. It was a very solemn speech because Antanas believed he would not be with his children much longer. His speech left them so tearful that another guest rose and showered congratulations on the couple to lighten the mood again.

Now the banquet began to break up. The real celebration of the evening was to begin. Chairs and babies were pulled out of the room. The company paired off quickly, and the whole room was soon in motion. There was a dance from home, and everyone joined in. At the climax the couples seized hands and began mad whirling.

After this, the revelers prepared for the *acziavimas*, the dance of the bride with every man. After each guest finished, he dropped into a hat a sum of money. The guests were expected to pay for this entertainment, and if they were proper guests,

---

3. Dede Grandfather, in Lithuanian

they would see that there was some money left over for the bride and groom.

The expenses of this entertainment were fearful to contemplate. They would certainly be over 200 dollars, maybe 300 dollars. There were men here who worked a year and did not see that much money. And then to spend that much in a single day! It was tragic—but it was so beautiful. These people had given up everything else, but they would not give up the wedding feast—that would be to acknowledge defeat. A man could live on the memory of his wedding all his days.

Endlessly the dancers swung round and round. Hour after hour this continued. The musicians had spent all their fine frenzy by now and played only one tune, wearily. All day Cousin Marija had been in a wonderful exaltation, and she would not let it go. When they tried to stop, Marija would emit a howl, shaking her fists. In sheer terror, the orchestra would strike up again. She drove on the dancers, pulling one way, pushing the other.

In the meantime, in another corner was an anxious conference between Teta[4] Elzbieta, Ona's stepmother; Dede Antanas; and a few friends of the family. The wedding feast is an unspoken contract in which everyone pays his share. But now they had come to the new country, and this responsibility was changing. It seemed there must be some poison in the air here. The young men would come in crowds and fill themselves, and sneak off without contributing any money. Now and then half a dozen would march out openly, making fun of you to your face. All these things were going on, and the family was helpless with dismay.

---

4. **Teta** Aunt, in Lithuanian

What made this all the more painful was that it was so hard on the few who had done their best. The delicatessen owner gave five dollars, and he had just mortgaged his store for two hundred dollars. The widow Aniele had three children and did washing at prices it would break your heart to know. She had given the entire profit of her chickens for several months.

More and more friends gathered. Finally there came Jurgis, and the story was told to him. He said quietly, "It is done, and there is no use in weeping, Teta Elzbieta." He saw the wild look of terror in Ona's eyes. "Little one," he said, in a low voice, "do not worry. I will pay them all somehow. I will work harder." That was what Jurgis always said. Ona took a deep breath; it was so wonderful to have a husband who could solve all problems and who was so big and strong!

It was now after midnight, and the dancers were dull and heavy. The merciless tune began again. "In the good old summertime!" It was three in the morning, and they had danced out all their joy, but no one had the power to think of stopping. At seven every one of them had to be in their workplace, and if one of them was a minute late he would be docked an hour's pay.

There was almost no farewell. Dede Antanas was asleep, and Teta Elzbieta and Marija were sobbing loudly. Then there was only the silent night, with the stars beginning to pale a little to the east. Jurgis, without a word, lifted Ona in his arms and strode out with her.

"You shall not go to work at Brown's today, little one," he whispered, as he climbed the stairs. She caught his arm in terror, gasping, "No! No! It will ruin us!"

But he answered her again: "Leave it to me; leave it to me. I will earn more money—I will work harder."

Chapter 2

Jurgis talked lightly about work because he was young. His fellow workers told him stories of the breaking down of men, there in the stockyards— stories to make your flesh creep—but Jurgis would only laugh. He had only been there four months, and he was a giant besides.

Jurgis was the sort of man the bosses liked. If he was working in a line of men, the line always moved too slowly for him. That was why he had been picked out. Jurgis had stood outside of Brown and Company, a meatpacking factory, not more than half an hour the second day of his arrival in Chicago, when he had been beckoned by one of the bosses. In vain would others tell him that men in that crowd had stood there a month. "Yes," he would say, "but what sort of men? Broken-down tramps."

"It is plain," they would answer, "that you have come from very far in the country." And this was the fact, for Jurgis had never seen a city before he set out to make his fortune in the world and earn his right to Ona. He had come from a part of Lithuania known as the Imperial Forest, a hunting preserve of the nobility. A very few peasants had settled in it; one of these was Jurgis's father, Antanas Rudkus. His other son was in the army, and his daughter's husband had bought the place when old Antanas decided to go with his son to America.

It was nearly a year and a half ago that Jurgis had met Ona. Jurgis had never expected to get married, but without having spoken a word to her, he found himself asking her parents to sell her to him for his wife. But Ona's father was a rich man, and felt his daughter was not for one such as Jurgis. Jurgis went home with a heavy heart and tried to forget her. Then he saw it would not do, and tramped the full fortnight's journey that lay between him and Ona.

He found that the girl's father had died and that his estate was tied up with creditors. Jurgis realized that the prize was within his reach. There was Ona's stepmother, Teta Elzbieta, and her four children and her brother Jonas. They were people of great consequence, it seemed to Jurgis. Ona could read and knew many things. But now the farm had been sold, and the family was adrift.

Ona might have married and left, but she would not. Jonas suggested they go to America, where a friend had gotten rich. In America, it was said, a man was free. They decided to leave the next spring. Jurgis sold himself to a contractor and worked on a railroad. Those were fearful days, but Jurgis withstood it and came out with 80 rubles sewed up in his coat.

So in the summertime they all set out for America. They were ten in all in the party, five adults and four children—and Ona who was a little of both. They had a hard time on the passage, which cost them a good deal of their precious money. The same thing happened in New York because, of course, they knew nothing about the country. The law says the rate card must be on the door of a hotel, but it does not say it shall be written in Lithuanian.

It was in the stockyards that Jonas's friend had gotten rich, and so to Chicago the party was headed.

They arrived in the city knowing that one word, "Chicago." They were pitiful in their helplessness. They wandered around, utterly lost, and were taken by a policeman to the station. In the morning an interpreter was found, and they were put on a trolley car and taught a new word—"stockyards."

They sat and stared out the window. The street seemed to run on forever. On each side was a row of wretched little two-story buildings. Here and there would be a great factory. As they traveled, they had noticed how it grew darker all the time and that the colors of things became dirtied with smoke and grime, the landscape hideous and bare. Along with the thickening smoke, they began to notice a strange, strong odor. They were not sure it was unpleasant, this odor; some might have called it sickening, but their taste in odors was not developed. They were only sure it was curious. Then a door was flung open, and a voice shouted—"Stockyards!"

They were left on the corner, staring. At the end of the street there were half a dozen chimneys, and leaping from them half a dozen columns of thick, oily, black smoke. The blackness spread in vast clouds overhead, uniting, and stretched as far as the eye could reach. Then the party became aware of another strange thing. It was a sound, made up of ten thousand little sounds. It was only with effort that they realized it was the distant lowing of ten thousand cattle, the grunting of ten thousand swine. They had arrived in Packingtown.[5]

They started up the street, when Jonas gave a cry. He bounded away and entered a shop over which was a sign: "J. Szedvilas, Delicatessen." When he came out, he was with a very stout gentleman in shirt-sleeves,

---

5. **Packingtown** an area in Chicago where animals are slaughtered and meat is processed

clasping Jonas by both hands. It was Szedvilas, the mythical friend who had made his fortune in America.

The two families happily greeted each other, for it had been years since Jokubas Szedvilas had met a man from his part of Lithuania. Jokubas could explain the pitfalls of this new world. He would take them to a woman who kept a boardinghouse; it was not choice, but it might do for the moment. Elzbieta responded that nothing could be too cheap. A few days in the land of high wages had made it clear to them that this was also the land of high prices.

Yet, when they saw the boardinghouse, they could not help but to recoil. There were half a dozen boarders to each room. The mattresses were spread on the floor in rows, and there was nothing else but a stove. It was unbelievably filthy.

"Tomorrow," Jurgis said, "I will get a job, and we can get a place of our own."

Later that afternoon he and Ona went to take a walk. There were no pavements; there were great hollows of stinking green water. This land was a dumping ground for the city's garbage. But as the sun went down on the scene, all the foul suggestions of the place were gone. It seemed a dream of wonder. As they came away, Jurgis was saying, "Tomorrow I shall go and get a job!"

Chapter 3

Jurgis had stood at Brown's not more than half an hour before one of the bosses noticed his form towering over the rest, and signaled to him. He had a job.

"Dekui, tamistai!" (Thank you, sir.) Jurgis turned away, and he gave a yell and a jump. There being no more to be done that day, the delicatessen owner Jokubas Szedvilas rushed forward to show his friend the sights of Packingtown.

It was still early morning, and a steady stream of employees were pouring through the gate. Jokubas hurried Jurgis on to where there was a stairway from which everything could be seen.

There was over a square mile of space in the yards, and more than half was occupied by cattle pens. And every pen was filled—so many cattle no one had ever dreamed existed in the world. Here and there galloped men on horseback. They would stop to inspect a bunch of cattle. The buyer would nod or drop his whip, and that would mean a bargain. All night this had been going on. Now the pens were full; by tonight they would be empty, and the same thing would be done again.

"By tonight, they will all be killed and cut up," said Jokubas, "and over there are more railroad tracks, where the cars come to take them away." The track brought ten million live creatures to be turned into food every year: cattle, hogs, and sheep.

One stood and watched, and little by little caught the drift of the tide of the packinghouses. Over here were groups of cattle being driven to the chutes.[6] In these chutes the stream of animals was continuous. It was uncanny to watch them—a very river of death. Over there were the chutes into which the hogs went. They climbed to the very top of the distant buildings, and their weight carried them back through the processes necessary to make them into pork.

"They don't waste anything here," said Jokubas,

---

6. **chutes**   inclined channels through which animals
   are passed

and then he laughed and said, "They use everything about the hog except the squeal."

Entering one of the buildings, a guide came to escort them. They made a great production of showing strangers through the plants, but Jokubas whispered that the visitors did not see any more than what the packers wanted them to see.

The tour group climbed a long series of stairways outside the building to the top of its six stories. Here was the chute, with its river of hogs all patiently toiling upward. Once there, they went into a room from which there is no returning for hogs. There was a great iron wheel that revolved. The men there had chains which they fastened onto the leg of the nearest hog, and then to one of the rings on the wheel. As the wheel turned, a hog was suddenly jerked off his feet and borne aloft. Another was swung up, and another, until there was a double line of them, kicking in frenzy—and squealing. It was too much for some of the visitors.

It was so businesslike that one watched it, fascinated. It was porkmaking by machinery. And yet somehow the most matter-of-fact person could not help thinking of the hogs; they were so innocent. They had done nothing to deserve this. Jurgis, as he turned to go on with the rest of the party, muttered, "I'm glad I'm not a hog!"

The carcass hog was scooped up by machinery and then it fell to the second floor. Looking down this room, one saw, creeping slowly, a line of dangling hogs, and for every yard there was a man working as if a demon were after him. At the end of the hog's progress every inch had been gone over several times, and then it was rolled into the chilling room.

The party descended to the next floor, where the waste materials were treated. Entrails[7] were scraped and cleaned for sausage casings[8]; scraps were boiled to make soap and lard. In other rooms men were splitting hogs, sending to one room hams, another sides of pork.

Then the party went across the street to where they did the killing of beef—where every hour they turned four or five hundred cattle into meat. All this work was done on one floor. It was a scene of intense activity.

Once crowded into pens, over the top of the pen leaned a "knocker" armed with a sledge hammer, waiting for a chance to deal a blow. The instant the animal had fallen, the animal was slid out to the "killing bed." Out of each pen rolled a steady stream of carcasses. The men worked with furious intensity. It was all highly specialized labor. First came the butcher to bleed them and leave blood a half-inch thick on the ground. There were men to cut the carcass, and men to split it, and men to gut it and scrape it clean inside. There were some with hoses which threw jets of boiling water on it, and others who removed the feet. In the end the finished beef was run into the chilling room.

The visitors were taken to the pickling rooms, and the salting rooms, and the canning rooms. There was a building to which the grease was piped and made into soap and lard, a building in which heads were made into glue. From knuckles and feet came such products as gelatin. They made violin strings from the foul-smelling entrails and when there was nothing else to be done with a thing, they made it into fertilizer.

The packing companies employed 30,000 men; the business supported directly 250,000 people in the neighborhood. Our friends listened open-mouthed. It

---

7. **entrails**   the internal organs, especially the intestines
8. **casings**   the cleaned intestines of a cow, used to contain processed meat in making sausage

seemed impossible that anything so stupendous could have been devised by man. All a man could do, it seemed to Jurgis, was to take a thing as great as this and do as he was told. And now he was admitted into the company—he was a part of it all!

Chapter 4

Promptly at seven the next morning Jurgis reported for work and followed the boss to the "killing beds." The work Jurgis had to do was simple. He swept smoking entrails into a trap, which was then closed. The place ran with steaming blood, and the stench was almost overpowering, but to Jurgis it was nothing. His whole soul was dancing with joy. He was at work at last! He was paid the fabulous sum of 17½ cents an hour!

At home, there was more good news. Jonas had been promised a job at the beginning of next week. Marija, with nothing but her two brawny arms and the word "job," had marched about Packingtown, and in the end she had reaped her reward. She had come to where cans of smoked beef were being painted and labeled. There a woman had told her to come the next day and she would have the chance to learn the trade of painting cans—a job that paid as much as two dollars a day.

Jurgis had determined that Teta Elzbieta should stay home and keep house and that Ona would help her. It would be a strange thing if a man like him could not support the family, with the board[9] of Jonas

---

9. board meals and lodging

and Marija. He would not hear of the children working; he had heard there were free schools in America for children.

So there was only old Dede Antanas. He had come to America as full of hope as the best of them, and now he was the chief problem worrying his son. Everyone said it was a waste of time for the old man to seek a job. But Dede Antanas had come home to hear of the others' triumph, and would smile bravely and say it would be his turn another day.

Jurgis had brought home an advertisement that had given him a wild idea. On the advertisement was a house, brilliantly painted, new and dazzling. "Why pay rent?" it asked in Polish, Lithuanian, and German. "Why not own your own home?"

Their good luck, the family felt, had given them the right to think of a home. Over this document the family pored long, while Ona spelled it out. It appeared that the house contained four rooms, besides a basement, and might be bought for 1,500 dollars, the lot and all. Of this, only 300 dollars had to be paid down, the balance being paid at the rate of 12 dollars a month. If they continued to pay rent, on the other hand, they might pay forever and be no better off.

They figured it out. If they combined their earnings, they would have enough money to make the first payment. It was, of course, something they would have to think about long and hard. And yet, if they were to do it, the sooner the better, for were they not paying rent all the time and living in the most horrible way besides? Jurgis was used to dirt, but that would not do for Ona. Jurgis was at a loss to understand why, with wages as high as they were, so many of these people should live the way they did.

The next day Marija was told to report the first of the week and learn the business of can-painter. She came home singing, and was just in time to join Ona and her stepmother as they set out to look at the house. That evening they made their report. The houses lay to the south. They were wonderful bargains, the gentleman had assured them. Anyone wishing to take advantage would have to be very quick. It had been arranged they would inspect the house on Sunday.

That was Thursday, and the rest of the week Jurgis cleared a dollar seventy-five every day. That was 45 dollars a month. Jurgis was not able to figure, except a simple sum, but Ona was like lightning at such things. She worked out that they should all together have 70 dollars a month—surely sufficient for the support of a family of ten.

On Sunday the entire party set out. At the house, the agent put in an appearance. He was smooth, elegantly dressed, and spoke their language. The house was one in a long row of frame dwellings. Ona's heart sank. The house was not as it was shown in the picture. Still, it was freshly painted. It was all new, the agent said, but he talked so fast they were confused. There were all sorts of things they had made up their minds to inquire about, but to press the matter would have seemed to be doubting him.

The house had a basement and an attic. The street was unpaved and unlighted. Inside were four rooms. The basement was but a frame. The attic was also unfinished, but there was no end to the advantages of the house, as the agent demonstrated. He showed them the kitchen with its running water, something Teta Elzbieta in her wildest dreams had never hoped to possess.

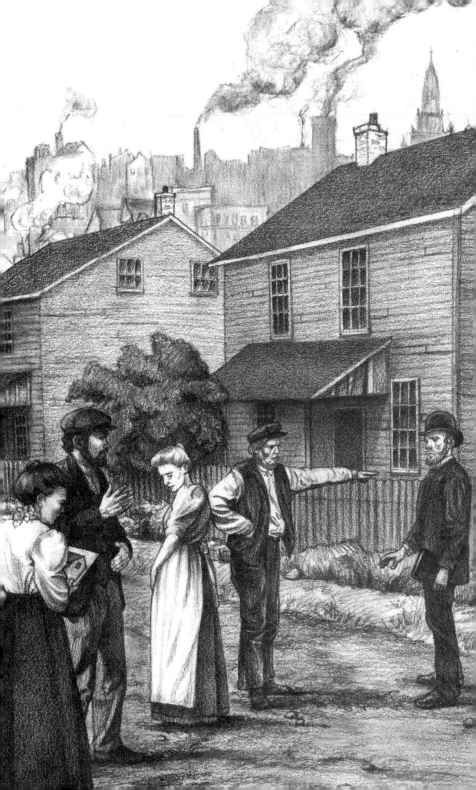

Still, they were peasant people, and they hung on to their money by instinct. It was agony to have to make up their minds. They had heard cruel stories of people who had been bankrupted in similar "buying a house" swindles. The house might be no good—how was a poorman to know? They could not stay where they were—they had to go somewhere. Also, the prospect of paying rent was just as hard to face. In the end, the decision was made by Jurgis. Others might have failed at buying a house, but he was not the failing kind. He took full responsibility. He would work all day, and all night, if need be; he would never rest until the house was paid for.

They were to come on the morrow, and the agent would have the papers all drawn up. Jurgis could not get a holiday, so there was nothing to be done but trust it to the women and to Szedvilas, the delicatessen owner.

Early in the morning they went. The women were quite pale with fright. The agent had the deed all ready, and invited them to read it. Szedvilas read on and on, during which the agent drummed on the desk. A horrible suspicion was dawning in Szedvilas's mind. This was no bill of sale—this deed provided only for renting the property!

The agent explained that that was usual. The agent began to explain again, but Elzbieta had in her mind the last warning of Jurgis: "If there is anything wrong, do not give him the money, but go out and get a lawyer."

The lawyer they found informed Szedvilas it was all perfectly regular. Szedvilas went on, asking one trembling question after another. When at last it came time for them to make up their minds, it was all

Teta Elzbieta could do to keep from bursting into tears. The eyes of everyone were on her, awaiting her decision; and at last, half blind with tears, she brought out the precious money and laid it on the table. The agent wrote a receipt and passed them the deed. They went into the street, Teta Elzbieta clutching her deed in her hand.

When Jurgis came home and heard their story, he was sure they had been swindled and were ruined. In the end he rushed out of the house and dragged Szedvilas to another lawyer. "He says it is all right," said Szedvilas. Jurgis, in his relief, sank down into a chair. He made Szedvilas translate question after question. Yes, they had really bought it. When the last rental payment was made, the house was all theirs. Then Jurgis covered his face with his hands, for there were tears in his eyes.

At home, Jurgis found Ona in a faint and the house in an uproar—for it had been believed by all that he had gone to murder the agent. Through the cruel night he would wake and hear Ona and her stepmother in the next room, sobbing softly to themselves.

Chapter 5

They had bought their home. They spent all their time thinking about it, and what furniture they were going to put into it. A person with such a task would not need to look far in Packingtown. He had only to read the signs to find information on anything a human creature could need.

Among all the signs, advertising everything from the Goliath Bunion Cure to the Eureka Two-fifty Shoe, one had caught the family's attention. "Feather your nest," it read—all the feathers for a four-room nest could be had for 75 dollars. Only a small part of the money need be paid—the rest one might pay with a few dollars every month. There was more agony and another paper for Elzbieta to sign. Then one night the furniture arrived.

The next day the men began carrying their belongings to their new home. The distance was over two miles, but Jurgis made two trips that night, each time with a huge pile of mattresses on his head. It was wonderful to see how fine the house looked; it was almost as exciting as the advertisement had described it. Ona was fairly dancing. It was a great day. Tired as they were, Jurgis and Ona sat up late, contented to hold each other and gaze in rapture about the room. They were going to be married as soon as they could get everything settled, and a little spare money put aside. This was to be their home—that little room yonder would be theirs!

It was a never-ending delight, the fixing up of this house. On Saturday night they came home with a great basket full of things and spread them out on the table while everyone stood around. There was sugar and salt and tea and crackers, and a can of lard and a milk pail, and a tack hammer, and a pound of nails.

The dining table was in the kitchen, and the dining room was used as the bedroom of Teta Elzbieta and four of her children. Ona and her cousin Marija dragged a mattress into the parlor and slept there. At a quarter past five every morning, Teta Elzbieta would have a great pot full of steaming black coffee ready. She would make oatmeal and bread and smoked sausages, and they would tramp away, stomachs full, to work.

At his new job, Jurgis stood and watched the men on the killing beds, marveling at their speed. The pace they set here called for every faculty[10] of a man—there was never one instant's rest for hand or eye or brain. Jurgis saw there were certain men paid high wages who worked like men possessed. This was called "speeding up the gang," and if any man could not keep up, there were hundreds outside begging to try.

It seemed to Jurgis that this was the first time he had ever really worked. Yet Jurgis rather enjoyed it. It was not the most pleasant work one could think of, but it was necessary work. So Jurgis thought, and so he spoke. Very much to his surprise, he found that this opinion got him into trouble, for the men here took a different view of the thing. He was quite dismayed when he found that most of the men *hated* their work. They hated the bosses and the whole place, the whole neighborhood. It was rotten, rotten as hell. When Jurgis would ask them what they meant, they would say, "Never mind, you stay here and see for yourself."

One of the first problems Jurgis ran into was the unions. He had no experience with unions and had to have it explained to him that, in a union, the men banded together to fight for their rights. Jurgis asked them what they meant by their rights, a question in which he was quite sincere, for he had not any idea of any rights except the right to hunt for a job and do as he was told when he got it. A union man came to enroll him. When Jurgis found out that meant he would have to part with some of his money, he froze

---

10. faculty ability or power

up. Little by little Jurgis gathered that the main thing the men wanted was to stop the "speeding up." There were some, they said, whom it was killing. But Jurgis had no sympathy with such ideas—he could do the work, and so could the rest of them, if they were good for anything.

Yet Jurgis, who dismissed the unfit as simply unworthy of the job, went about all day sick at heart because of his poor old father, who was begging for a chance to earn his bread. Old Antanas had been a worker ever since he was a child. He had been into every building in Packingtown by this time, and everywhere they had ordered him out, sometimes with curses.

So there was a fine crack in Jurgis's faith in things as they were. The crack widened when Dede Antanas was hunting for a job—and grew wider still when he finally got it. One day the old man came home in a state of excitement. A man in the pickle rooms at Durham's had asked what he would be willing to pay to get a job. Jurgis asked a friend about it.

Giving money to a boss in exchange for work was common enough, the friend said. It was simply some boss who proposed to add to his own income. Warming to the subject, the friend went on to explain the situation. Durham's was owned by a man who wanted to make money and did not care how he did it. Underneath this man there were managers, each one driving the man below him and trying to squeeze as much work out of him as possible. The men of the same rank were pitted against each other, and every man lived in terror of losing his job if another produced more than he. There was no loyalty or decency; there was not even any honesty.

Like all the rest, the friend said, Jurgis had thought he would rise and become a skilled man; but he would soon discover his error—for nobody rose in Packingtown by doing good work. The man who told tales, *he* would rise; but the man who did his work— why, they would "speed him up" until they had worn him out. Then they would throw him in the gutter.

Jurgis went home with his head buzzing. It could not be so. His friend was a puny chap, and so he had been left behind in the race, and that was why he was so unhappy. And yet so many strange things kept coming to Jurgis's notice every day!

Old Antanas went and found the man who had spoken to him and promised to bring him a third of all he earned. He was put to work in Durham's cellars that day. It was a "pickle room," where there was never a dry spot to stand on, and so he had to spend nearly his first week's earnings on a pair of heavy-soled boots. His job was to go around all day with a long-handled mop, swabbing the floor. Except that it was damp and dark, it was not an unpleasant job in the summer.

Now Antanas Rudkus was a mild man, and Jurgis found it a striking confirmation of what the men all said, that his father had been at work only two days before he came home as bitter as any. The family listened in wonder as he told them how he was working in the room where the men prepared the beef for canning. The beef had lain in vats of chemicals, and men speared it out and emptied the vat on the floor. They set Antanas with his mop slopping the "pickle" into a hole where it was caught and used over and over, forever.

Jonas and Marija also came with tales. Marija was beside herself with triumph over the money she was making as a painter of cans. But one day she walked home with a pale little woman who told her how Marija had chanced to get her job. She had taken the place of an Irishwoman who had been working in the factory for over 15 years. She had a little boy; he was a cripple, and all she had in the world to love. The Irishwoman had consumption,[11] and all day long you could hear her coughing. Marija's friend did not know what had become of the poor creature. The forelady could not stop for sick people, she explained.

Jonas, too, had gotten his job by the misfortune of some other person. Jonas worked pushing a truck loaded with hams from the smoke rooms to an elevator. Each truck was made of iron, and heavy, and had a load of more than a quarter ton. The man who had the job before Jonas had been jammed against the wall by one and crushed in a horrible manner.

All these were sinister tales, but trifles next to what Jurgis saw with his own eyes. Any man who knows anything about butchering knows that the flesh of a cow that is about to give birth, or has just calved, is not fit for food. A good many came through, and whoever noticed would tell the boss. The boss would start up a conversation with the government inspector, and so in a very short time, the carcass of the cow would be cleaned out. It was Jurgis's task to slide them into the trap, calves and all, and on the floor below they took these cows and butchered them for meat.

One day Jurgis was ordered to remain and do some special work. It was almost dark, and the government inspectors were all gone. That day they had killed about four thousand cattle. Some had broken legs, and there were some that had died, and they were all to be disposed of here in darkness and silence. The

---

11. consumption   tuberculosis, a disease of the lungs that causes a person to waste away

gang proceeded to handle them with an air of businesslike nonchalance[12] which said plainer than words that it was an everyday routine. Jurgis saw these cows go into the chilling rooms with the rest of the meat. When he got home he was in a very somber mood, having begun to see at last how those might be right who laughed at him for his faith in America.

Chapter 6

Jurgis and Ona were very much in love. It was now well into their second year in America, and Jurgis judged everything by whether it helped or hindered his ability to get married. The marriage would have been at once, if they had had their way. But this would mean they would have to do without any wedding feast, and to Teta Elzbieta especially, the very suggestion was unthinkable. Elzbieta had grown up on a big estate, with servants, and might have been a lady but for the fact that there had been nine daughters and no son in the family. Even so, she knew what was decent, and clung to her traditions with desperation. They were not going to lose all social position, even if they had come to be unskilled laborers in Packingtown. They must not give up what was right for a little money.

The cost of the wedding feast would, of course, be returned, but the problem was to raise the money even temporarily. Evening after evening Jurgis and Ona would sit and figure the expenses. They could not possibly manage it for less than 200 dollars, and

---

12. **nonchalance** having an air of easy unconcern

could not hope to raise this sum in less than four months. So Ona began thinking of seeking employment, saying that she might be able to take two months off the time. They were just beginning to adjust themselves to this necessity when a thunderbolt fell, scattering their hopes.

About a block away lived another Lithuanian family; our friends struck up an acquaintance with them. One evening they came over for a visit, and the conversation turned to the neighborhood and its history. A neighbor, Grandmother Majauszkiene, proceeded to recite a string of horrors that froze their blood. As she mumbled the grim story through her toothless gums, she seemed a very old witch to them. She talked about starvation, sickness, and death as other people might about weddings and holidays.

In the first place the house they had bought was not new at all; it was about 15 years old, and there was nothing new but the paint. The house was built by a company that existed to make money by swindling poor people. The family had paid 1,500 dollars for it, and it had not cost the builders 500 dollars when it was new. The family could take her word as to the trouble they would have, for she and her son had bought their house the same way. They had fooled the company, however, and paid for the house.

She saw that her friends were puzzled by this. They did not see how paying for the house was "fooling the company." The houses were sold with the idea that the people who bought them would not be able to pay for them, the Grandmother said. When they failed—if only by a single month—they would lose the house and all they had paid on it. Why, since it had been built, no fewer than four families had tried to buy it and failed.

First, there had been the Germans. Next were the Irish, then the Bohemians, and after them the Poles. Now the Lithuanians were giving way to the Slovaks. Who were poorer than the Slovaks, Grandmother Majauszkiene had no idea, but the packers would find them. By and by the people would have their revenge, though, for things were getting beyond human endurance, and the people would rise up and murder the packers. Grandmother Majauszkiene was a Socialist[13] or some strange thing.

They called her back to the story of the house. The German family had been a good sort, but the father had been killed in an elevator accident at Durham's.

Then had come the Irish. They were always behind with their rent, but they belonged to the "War Whoop League,"[14] and if you belonged to that, you could never be arrested for anything. The father had gone all to ruin with the drink, though; one of the sons had kept the payments up, but then he got sick with consumption. In those days, the packers had worked all but the babies. When they looked puzzled, she explained that it was against the law for children to work before they were 16. But they had been thinking of letting little Stanislovas go to work, they told her. No need to worry, Grandmother Majasuzkiene said— people only had to lie about the ages of their children.

To get back to the house, it was the woman of the next family who died. After she died the man would work all day and leave the children to shift for themselves. At the end, the children were there three days alone, before it was discovered that the father

---

13. **Socialist** one who believes in a system of government in which the people own the means of production and the distribution of goods
14. **War Whoop League** a political club whose members were protected by the politicians who ran it

was dead. A wounded steer had broken loose and mashed him against a pillar.

So this grim woman went on with her tale of horrors. Then they asked why the families had been unable to pay. "It is 12 dollars a month; but that does not include interest," she said.

They stared at her. "Interest!" they cried. "But we don't have to pay any interest!"

And for this she laughed at them. "You are like all the rest. They trick you and eat you alive. They never sell the houses without interest. Get your deed, and see."

The old lady, who could read English, ran over the lease. "Yes," she said, "here it is. You have to pay them seven dollars next month, as well as the twelve dollars."

It was sickening, a nightmare. They wished the old woman would be still; her voice sounded like the croaking of some dismal raven. Suddenly, Teta Elzbieta broke the silence with a wail, and Marija began to sob.

Somehow they got rid of their guest. The children woke, and found that something was wrong, and cried. By seven o'clock Ona and her stepmother were standing at the door of the office of the agent. He was deeply pained, he said. He had thought they understood they had to pay interest.

Ona went down to the yards and told Jurgis. He took the news with little emotion. He made his usual answer: "I will work harder." But this upset their wedding plans; now it would be necessary for Ona and Stanislovas to work. The family would have to help as it could.

So Ona set out to hunt for work. Marija came home saying she had met a girl who might know a place; only the forelady was the kind that takes bribes. Jurgis was not surprised at this by now. Ona reported that the forelady might be able to put her to work sewing covers on hams. In the end Ona, with a ten-dollar bill in her palm, had another interview with the forelady.

Stanislovas now had a certificate that said he was two years older than he was. It chanced that Durham's had a wonderful new lard machine. The lard came in little jets, like beautiful, wriggling, snow-white snakes of unpleasant odor. Each stopped automatically, and the machine turned. To attend to this and fill the hundreds of cans per hour, two human creatures were necessary.

And so little Stanislovas was shown how to place a lard can. Hour after hour, year after year, it was fated that he should stand thinking never a thought save for the setting of lard cans. Half the year he would never know what the sun looked like on weekdays. And for this, at the end of the week, he would carry home three dollars.

And meantime, Jurgis and Ona were again calculating. The wages of Stanislovas would leave them about as they had been before! It would be fair to say the boy was delighted with his work and the idea of earning money; and also that Ona and Jurgis were very much in love with each other.

Chapter 7

In the fall the family had money enough for Jurgis and Ona to be married. They hired a hall. In the end, they were left with over 100 dollars of debt. It was a bitter experience and plunged them into despair.

They wondered if ever any love had been so crushed and trampled!

Over them cracked the lash of want. The day after the wedding Ona was scarcely able to stand from exhaustion, but if she were to lose her job they would be ruined. Jurgis lost his temper very little. If he did at all, he controlled himself because of Ona. She was too good for him, he told himself. He had to protect her, to do battle for her against the horror he saw about them. He would wrap his arms around her and try to hide her from the world.

He had learned the ways of things. You did not give feasts to other people; you waited for them to give feasts to you. The great corporation that employed you lied to you. There were many dangers, in which the odds were all against them. How could they know there was no sewer to their house and that the drainage of 15 years resulted in a cesspool[15] under it? How could they know the milk was watered down? How could they know their sugar was doctored?

And then there was old Antanas. He worked in a dark, unheated cellar, so his cough grew worse every day. His feet were soaked in chemicals, and it was not long before they had eaten through his new boots. Sores broke out on his feet and grew worse and worse. He asked other workers about it and found out that everyone got ill, sooner or later. The sores would never heal if he did not quit. Yet old Antanas would not quit. He went on limping and coughing until at last he fell to pieces. They carried him to a dry place and at night two men helped him home.

Though he tried it every morning until the end, he never got up again. And one night he had a choking fit, and a little river of blood came out of his mouth.

---

15. cesspool   a covered hole or pit for waste or sewage

The family, wild with terror, sent for a doctor, only to be told there was nothing to be done. At last one morning they found him stiff and cold. Though it nearly broke Teta Elzbieta's heart, they could afford few of the decencies of a funeral.

Now the dreadful winter was upon them. There came biting winds and blizzards. Sooner or later came the day when the unfit did not report for work. The new hands to replace them arrived by the thousands. All day long the packinghouses were crowded with starving men. Sometimes their faces froze, but still they came, for they had no place else to go.

One may imagine how the women and children fared in the cold. One morning the little boy who worked with Stanislovas came in and began screaming with pain. A man began rubbing his ears, and as they were frozen stiff, it took only two or three rubs to break them off. As a result, little Stanislovas developed a terror of the cold. Threats did no good, and in the end he always went with Jurgis and came home with him again.

There was no heat in the killing beds. You were apt to be covered with blood, and it would freeze solid. The cruelest thing of all was that those who used knives were unable to wear gloves. Their hands would grow numb, and, of course, there would be accidents.

They might have put up with all this reasonably well, if only there had been a place where they might eat. Jurgis had to eat his dinner amid the stench in which he worked or rush, as did all his companions, to the saloon. In the saloons there was always a warm stove and food, but to stay you had to drink. From the saloons Jurgis was saved because of Ona. At night he would go straight home.

Home was not very attractive. They had only been able to buy one small stove. They could feel the cold as it crept through the cracks, reaching for them. The next day would be another day of toil, another day a little nearer to death.

Chapter 8

It was then that the great adventure befell Marija. The victim was Tamoszius, who played the violin. He was petite and frail, and Marija could have carried him off under one arm. Perhaps that was why she fascinated him. The night of the wedding he had hardly taken his eyes off her, and he had got into the habit of coming to pay her visits on Sunday afternoons. Tamoszius would never say more than a half-dozen words, but finally Jurgis would clap him on the back, crying, "Give us a tune." And he would get out his fiddle and play, and all the while his gaze would be fixed on Marija, until she would turn red and lower her eyes.

Once he asked Marija to go with him to a party, where he would play. Marija accepted, to his great delight—after which he never went anywhere without her. One night, Tamoszius put down his violin and spoke his heart; and Marija clasped him in her arms. They would sit for hours in the kitchen, blissfully happy.

They were planning to be married in the spring, and fix up the attic of the house, and live there. Marija had become an expert can painter. Her friends would shake their heads; one could not count on good fortune forever. But Marija went on dreaming. When the crash came, her grief was painful to see. The factory shut down! That was all there was to it—her job was gone!

The holiday rush was over, the girls said. There was always a slack. You were crazy with delight, making 14 dollars a week, but then you had to spend it all to stay alive.

Marija set out to search for a job, but with all the girls hunting for work, she did not find any. The men also felt the effects of the slump. The packinghouses ran for shorter and shorter hours. The men had to be ready for work at seven o'clock, but they would perhaps not have a thing for the men to do until late in the afternoon.

Some weeks Jurgis went home with pay for no more than two hours' work—about 35 cents. Sometimes cars of cattle would pull-in late in the day; then would come into play the ironclad rule that the cattle must be killed the day they arrived. On Christmas Eve Jurgis worked till nearly one in the morning.

All this was bad, and yet it was not the worst. Jurgis had once scoffed at the idea of these huge companies cheating; now he could appreciate the irony that their size enabled them to do just that. They did not pay for any part of an hour. A man might work 50 minutes, but if there was no work to fill out the hour, there was no pay.

Jurgis was no longer perplexed when he heard men talk about fighting for their rights. When the Irishman from the union came a second time, he received him in a far different spirit. A wonderful idea, it now seemed to Jurgis, that by joining together they might conquer the packers! Before another month, all the working members of his family had union cards.

But ten days after she joined, Marija's factory closed. Why had the union not prevented it? At a union meeting Marija made a speech, telling what she thought of the packers, and the hall rang with her terrible voice. Then the meeting gathered itself together and discussed the election of a recording secretary.

Jurgis never missed a union meeting. The speakers were all desperate to make changes, as was Jurgis, for he understood that a fight was on. Jurgis had sworn to trust no man, but here he discovered he had brothers and allies. The struggle became a kind of crusade. Here was a new religion—one that took every fiber of him. He went out as a missionary to spread the gospel of Brotherhood.

Chapter 9

One consequence of the discovery of the union was that Jurgis wanted to learn English. When he learned of a free night school he went and enrolled. After that, every evening he got home from the yards in time, he would go to the school.

The union had made another great difference in him—it made him pay attention to the country. The union, where every man had a say, was Jurgis's first experience with democracy. Where he had come from there was no politics—in Russia the government was an affliction like the lightning and the hail. When Jurgis had first come here he had heard people say this was a free country—but what did that mean? He found that here, as in Russia, there were rich men who owned everything.

One day a man came who asked Jurgis if he would like to become a United States citizen. It would not cost, and he would get half a day off, with pay. Jurgis was glad to accept. He and the other men had a merry time, with plenty of beer, and each man took an oath, and became a citizen. On election day, the packinghouses posted a notice that men who voted might stay away until nine. The same man took Jurgis and the rest and showed them how to mark a ballot, and gave them each two dollars.

The union men explained to Jurgis that there were two rival sets of grafters[16] and that the one who got elected to office was the one who bought the most votes. The ruler of the district was the Democratic boss, an Irishman named Mike Scully. He was enormously rich. He owned the dump and the brick factory. A note from him was good for a job at the packinghouses, and he employed a great many men himself. This gave him many friends—all of whom he had gotten into the "War Whoop League." The man who had taken Jurgis to become a citizen was a member. Even the packers were in awe of him, the men said. It gave them pleasure to believe this, for Scully stood as the people's man.

The city had threatened to make the packers cover over "Bubbly Creek," until Scully came to their aid. All the drainage from the packinghouses emptied into it, so it was really an open sewer. The grease and chemicals poured into it underwent strange transformations, which gave it its name.

There were things even stranger than this,

---

16. grafters people who get money in illegal ways

according to the gossip of the men. The people of Chicago saw the government inspectors in Packingtown and took that to mean they were protected from diseased meat. They did not understand that the inspectors had been appointed at the request of the packers, and that they were paid by the United States government to certify that all the diseased meat was kept within the state. It was only meat sold in interstate commerce—to other states and foreign countries—that the federal inspectors cared about. There were only three inspectors for the meat that was to be sold within the city and state, and all of these were hired by the local political machine!

When one of these inspectors had seen that carcasses with deadly ptomaine poisoning were to be sold in the city, he insisted that these carcasses be injected with kerosene so they could not be eaten. He was ordered to resign the same week. The packers felt so much righteous anger at this that they insisted that the mayor abolish the entire city inspection force. Since then, there had been no interference of any kind.

Jurgis heard of these things little by little. Every day he heard of new swindles and new crimes. There was, for instance, a Lithuanian cattle butcher who worked at the plant where Marija worked. He killed animals for canning only. It seemed there must be agencies all over the country to hunt out old and diseased cattle to be canned. There were cattle that were covered with boils, and it was a nasty job killing these, for when you plunged your knife into them the boils would burst, splashing foul-smelling stuff into your face. When a man's hands were steeped in blood, how was he ever to wipe his face?

One evening, Jurgis sat talking to a fellow who worked at Durham's. He told Jurgis they advertised a mushroom-catsup, and the men who made it did not know what a mushroom looked like. They advertised "potted chicken," and the things that went into the mixture were pork fat, beef suet, and beef hearts. Any inventor of an imitation meat could make a fortune from old man Durham, said the man, but it was hard to think of anything new in a place where so many people had been working for so long.

There was another interesting set of statistics that a person might have gathered in Packingtown—the various afflictions of the workers. The visitor might be skeptical about the swindles, but he could not be skeptical about these afflications—one look at an injured worker was evidence enough.

There were the men in the pickle rooms, where let a man so much as scrape a finger, and he might have a sore that would kill him. All the joints in his fingers might be eaten by acid, one by one. Of those who used knives, you could scarcely find a person who had the use of his thumb. Time and time again the base of it had been slashed, till it was a mere lump of flesh against which the man pressed the knife to hold it.

There were the beef-luggers, who carried 200-pound quarters of beef, and that wore out the most powerful men in a few years. There were the wool pluckers, whose hands went to pieces even sooner than the hands of the pickle men. The pelts of the sheep had to be painted with acid to loosen the wool, and then the pluckers had to pull out this wool with their bare hands, till the acid had eaten their fingers off. There were those who made the tins for the canned meat, and their hands, too, were a maze of cuts, and each cut represented a chance for blood poisoning. Some worked at the stamping machines, and it was very seldom that a man could work long there at the pace that was set and not give out, forget himself, and have a part of his hand chopped off.

Worst of all were the fertilizer men and those in the cooking rooms. These people could not be shown to the visitor. The odor of a fertilizer man would scare any ordinary visitor at a hundred yards. As for the men who worked near the open vats, their peculiar trouble was that they fell into the vats. When they were fished out, there was not enough left to be worth showing. Sometimes they would be overlooked for days, till all but their bones had gone into the world as Durham's Pure Leaf Lard!

Chapter 10

During the early part of the winter the family had enough money to live, but when the earnings of Jurgis fell from nine or ten dollars to five or six, there was no longer anything to spare. The spring came and found them still living from hand to mouth, with literally not a month's wages between them and starvation. Marija was in despair, for there was no word about the canning factory reopening, and her savings were almost gone.

There seemed no end to the things they had to buy. Once their water pipes froze and burst, and a plumber came with a helper and charged for the work and for all sorts of materials and extras. And then when they went to pay their January installment on the house, the agent terrified them by asking them if they had the insurance attended to yet. It would cost seven dollars, the man said, and that night came Jurgis, grim and determined, asking the agent to inform him, once and for all, of all the expenses for which they were liable. The deed was signed now, he said, with sarcasm proper to the new way of life he had learned. The fellow wasted no time in protests, but read him the deed. All together, 26 dollars a year, unless the city decided to put in a sidewalk or a sewer, which might be another 50 dollars all together.

Jurgis went home; it was a relief to know the worst. He saw how they had been plundered, but there was no turning back. They could only make the fight and win.

When the spring came, they no longer had to pay for coal, but then, too, the warm weather brought trials of its own. In spring there were cold rains and mud so deep wagons would sink into their hubs. Later came the summer, with its stifling heat, and the killing beds became a hell. With the hot weather descended a plague of flies. The houses would all be black with them, and there was no escaping.

Perhaps the summer suggests to you thoughts of the country, of green fields and sparkling lakes. It had no such suggestion to the people of the yards. They never saw any green thing. The blue waters of Lake Michigan lay four or five miles east, but for all the good it did them it might have been the Pacific Ocean. They were tied to the great packing machine for life.

In late spring the canning factory started up again, and once more Marija was heard to sing. It was not for long, for a month later she lost her job. Marija insisted it was because of her activity in the union. The known facts were that before the factory closed,

Marija had been cheated out of her pay for 300 cans. The woman who counted the number of cans sometimes made mistakes, and you had to make the best of it, but Marija did not understand this. She called the woman names, and the woman began to dislike her. The third time she made a mistake, Marija went on the warpath and finally took the matter to the superintendent. He said he would look into it, and when she asked again, he frowned, and the third time ordered her back to work with a passion. That afternoon the forelady told her that her services were no longer required. At first Marija could not believe it; then she grew furious, and in the end she sat down and wailed.

It was especially hard this time, for Ona was to have a baby before long, and Jurgis was trying to save up money for this. He was determined that Ona must have a doctor—the cheapest they could find would charge them 15 dollars.

Marija only had about 25 dollars left. Day after day she wandered about begging for a job, but this time without hope of finding it. She learned her lesson this time—the poor creature—that when you have a job in Packingtown, you hang on to it, come what may.

Marija stopped paying dues to the union, and cursed herself that she had ever been dragged into one. She had just about made up her mind that she was a lost soul, and then she got a job as a "beef-trimmer." The boss saw that she had strong muscles, and paid her a little more than half of what he had been paying the man before her.

Her work was to trim the meat of diseased cattle. She was shut up in rooms where the people seldom saw daylight. She worked till she trembled in every nerve and gave herself a poisoned wound—that was the new life that unfolded before Marija. And as for Tamoszius—well, they had waited a long time, and they could wait longer. Day by day the music of his violin became more heartbreaking, and Marija would sit with her hands clasped and her cheeks wet and her body atremble. She heard in the melodies the voices of the unborn generations that cried out in her for life.

Marija's lesson came just in time to save Ona from a similar fate. Ona, too, was dissatisfied and with far more reason than Marija. She did not tell half her story at home because she was afraid of what Jurgis might do. Ona knew her forelady did not like her. In the end Ona learned it was because the forelady was a kept woman who ran a bawdyhouse, and ran her department along with it. Sometimes decent girls were let go to make room for women from the house. Ona would not have stayed a day, but for starvation. She understood now that the reason the forelady hated her was because she was a decent married girl. But there was no place a girl could go in Packingtown if she were particular about things of this sort.

One day Ona stayed home, and Jurgis had the doctor come, and she had her baby. It was a big boy. Jurgis would gaze at the baby by the hour, unable to believe it was real. The coming of the baby was a decisive event for Jurgis. It made him irrevocably[17] a family man. There was nothing he cared for so much as to sit and look at the baby.

Jurgis had, alas, little time to see his baby. When he came home the baby would be asleep, and then in the morning there was no time to look at him, so really the only time he had was on Sunday. This was more cruel yet for Ona, who should have stayed home and

---

17. irrevocably not possible to change as a protest

nursed him. But Ona had to go to work and leave Teta Elzbieta to feed him the pale blue poison the grocery called milk. After a week she had gone back to work; if she waited longer she might find that the dreadful forelady had put someone in her place. That would be a greater problem now than ever, on account of the baby. They must all work harder now on his account. The baby must not grow up to suffer as they had.

Chapter 11

During the summer, Jurgis made more money. However, he did not make as much as the summer before because the packers hired more workers. Soon they would have all the floating labor of Chicago trained, and what a cunning trick that was! The men would teach enough hands so that the factory could keep running even if there was a strike.[18]

Meanwhile, the speeding up grew more savage. It was said the speed at which the hogs moved was increased a little each day. In piecework they required the same work in less time, and paid the same wages. Girls in canning jobs were fairly desperate; their wages had gone down by a third in the past two years.

Jurgis and Ona heard these stories with dismay. There had been rumors that a big house was going to cut its unskilled men to 15 cents an hour and he knew if this were done, his turn would come soon. Jurgis had learned by now that Packingtown was not many firms, but one great firm, called the Beef Trust. Every week the managers got together and compared prices

---

18. strike   a temporary halt of normal work activity, meant

and wages. There was one pay scale for all the workers in the yards. Jurgis was told they also fixed the price of all the dressed meat in the country, but that he did not care about.

The only one who was not afraid was Marija, who was getting to be a skilled beef trimmer. Jurgis and Ona paid her back what they owed her, and she began to build up a bank account.

Now chill winds began to warn them that winter was coming again. They had not had time to get ready for it, but still it came. The prospect struck fear into the heart of Jurgis, for Ona was not fit to face the snow this year.

It was the week before Christmas that the first storm came. For four days the cars did not run, and for the first time in his life, Jurgis knew what it was to really struggle. The first morning they set out two hours before dawn, Ona tossed on his shoulder like a sack of meal. The thermometer stood below zero; in some of the drifts the snow was nearly to his armpits. When he came to Durham's, he was staggering and almost blind.

A time of peril on the killing beds was when a steer broke loose. Sometimes they would dump an animal out on the floor before it was fully stunned, and it would get on its feet and run amuck. There would be a yell of warning—the men would drop everything and dash for the nearest pillar. In the wintertime the room would be so full of steam you could not make anything out five feet in front of you. And then the floor boss would come rushing up with a rifle and begin blazing away!

It was during one of these confused struggles that Jurgis was injured. At first he hardly noticed it, it was such a slight accident—in leaping out of the way he had turned his ankle. There was a twinge of pain, but Jurgis was used to pain. When he started to walk home, however, he realized it was hurting a great deal. The next morning he could not get into his shoe. He wrapped his foot in old rags, and hobbled out. By noon the pain was so great it made him faint, and after a couple of hours he had to tell the boss. The company doctor examined the foot and told Jurgis to go home to bed, adding that he had probably laid himself up for months by his folly. The injury was not one for which the company could be held responsible.

Jurgis got home somehow, scarcely able to see from the pain, and with an awful terror in his soul. Elzbieta bandaged his injured foot, and tried hard not to let him see her dismay. The others, too, put on a cheerful face, saying that it would only be a week or two before he could return to work.

When they had gotten him to sleep, however, they sat by the kitchen fire and talked it over in frightened whispers. Jurgis had only about 60 dollars in the bank. There was the rent, and money owed on the furniture, the insurance, and every month money due for coal. Deep snows would come again, and who would carry Ona to her work now?

The bitterness of this was the daily food of Jurgis. He knew the family might starve. It was almost maddening for a fighter like him to lie there helpless. It was like seeing the world fall away from underneath his feet. It might be true, after all, what others had told him about life, that the best powers of a man might not be equal to it! The thought was like an icy hand at his heart.

Ona was now making about 30 dollars a month, and Stanislovas about 13. The board of Jonas and Marija was about 45 dollars. Deducting from this the rent, interest, and installments on the furniture, they had left 60 dollars, and deducting the coal, they had 50. They did without everything human beings could go without. They dressed in old and ragged clothing, and when the children's shoes wore out, they tied them up with string. Still they could not stay alive on 50 dollars a month. If only they could have gotten pure food, and at fair prices, or known what to get—but they were so pitifully ignorant! Every week they made inroads into Ona's pitiful little bank account. The account was in her name, so it was possible for her to keep this a secret from her husband.

It would have been better if Jurgis had been really ill; if he had not been able to think. All he could do was lie there and toss from side to side. It was the one consolation of Jurgis's long imprisonment that now he had time to look at his baby. Jurgis would lie on one elbow and watch him by the hour. Then little Antanas would open his eyes—how he would smile! So Jurgis would forget his troubles because he was in a world where there was a thing so beautiful as the smile of little Antanas, and because such a world must be good at the heart of it.

Chapter 12

For three weeks Jurgis never got up from bed. The swelling would not go down, and the pain continued. At the end of that time, however, he could contain himself no longer and began trying to persuade himself that he was better. Three or four days later he declared that he was going back to work. He limped to the cars and got to Brown's. Every now and then the pain would force Jurgis to stop work, but he stuck it out until an hour before closing, when he was forced to acknowledge that he could not go on without fainting. It almost broke his heart, and he stood against a pillar, weeping like a child.

So they put him to bed again and sent for the doctor. He had twisted a tendon out of place and could never have gotten well without attention. The doctor wrenched at his swollen ankle and told him he would have to lie quiet for two months, and that if he went to work before that time he might lame himself for life.

Three days later there was a heavy snowstorm, and Jonas and Marija and Ona and little Stanislovas set out before daybreak. About noon Ona and the boy came back, the boy screaming with pain, his fingers frozen. They had given up trying to get to the yards. Ona was quite certain she had lost her job, but then found that the forelady herself had failed to come.

Perhaps the worst consequence of the long siege[19] was that they lost Jonas. One Saturday night he did not come home. Most probable was the theory that he had deserted them and gone on the road, seeking happiness. He had long been discontented, and not

---

19. siege a prolonged period of suffering

without cause. He paid good board, but there was never enough to eat. Jonas was not a hero—he was simply an old fellow who liked a good supper and to sit by the fire and smoke his pipe in peace before he went to bed. Here there was no room by the fire, and the kitchen had seldom been warm enough for comfort. What was more likely than that the wild idea of escaping had occurred to him?

But now the family's income was cut down by more than one-third, and they were worse off then ever. They were borrowing money from Marija and spoiling her hopes of marriage and happiness.

So it was decided that three more of Elzbieta's children would have to leave school. One morning Kotrina, 13, Vilimas, 11, and Nikalojus, 10, were given a quarter and a sausage in a roll and sent out to make their way to the city and learn to sell newspapers. After a week of being in the wrong place and being thrashed, and having their money stolen, they learned the ways of the trade. They began to come home with as much as 40 cents a day.

Now that it was warmer and there was enough money to get along from week to week, Jurgis had gotten used to lying around the house. Ona tried not to destroy his peace of mind, but it pained her that he did not notice her misery. And when they talked, they had only their worries to talk of—it was hard, in such a life, to keep any sentiment alive.

In April Jurgis was told by the doctor that he might go back to work. The foreman had not kept his place, though, and Jurgis joined the mob of the unemployed outside. This time, Jurgis was no longer the finest-looking man in the crowd. He was thin and miserable, and there were hundreds who looked just like him, and who had been begging for work for months. This was a critical time in Jurgis's life, and if he had been a weaker man he would have gone the way the rest did, racing into the saloons. Jurgis was saved from this desire mainly because he carried with him always the pitiful little face of his wife. He must get work!

But there was no work for him. He sought out the union and begged them to speak a word for him. He went to everyone he knew. Then there was nothing more for him but to go with the crowd and look eager.

The bitterness of all this was that Jurgis saw so plainly the meaning of it. In the beginning he had been strong, and had gotten a job the first day; now he was damaged, and they did not want him. They had worn him out, and now they had thrown him away! Jurgis found out that the other unemployed men had the same experience. They were simply the worn-out parts of the great packing machine. They would get their job back only when the accident was one for which the firm was liable. The firm would first get a slippery lawyer to get a worker to sign away his claims. But if the injured worker was too smart for that, he would get the company to promise him he should always be provided with work. This promise they would keep—for two years. Two years was the statute of limitations, and after that the victim could not sue.

What happened to a man after any of these things depended on circumstances. If he were highly skilled, he would have enough to tide him over. The best men, the "splitters," made five or six dollars a day in the rush seasons, but there were only half a dozen in each place. An unmarried man could save, if he did not drink, and was absolutely selfish—that is, he paid no attention to the demands of his old parents, or of his little brothers and sisters, or of the people who might be starving to death next door.

Chapter 13

While he was looking for work there was a dark shadow hanging over Jurgis. There are all stages of being out of work in Packingtown, but there is a place that waits for the lowest man—the fertilizer plant!

The men talked about it in awe-stricken whispers. There were some things even worse than starving to death. Jurgis would debate with himself. As poor as they were, would he dare to refuse any work? Would he dare to go home and eat bread earned by Ona, weak as she was, knowing he had not had the nerve to take a job? And yet a glimpse into the fertilizer works would send him away shuddering. He would do his duty and make out an application—but surely he was not required to hope for success!

To this part of the yard came waste products. Here they dried the bones. In suffocating cellars, you might see people bending over whirling machines, doomed, every one, to die within a certain time, breathing their lungs full of fine dust.

On top of this were the rooms where they dried the waste. This dried material they would grind to a powder. A farmer would buy a ton of fertilizer. For several days the fields would have a strong odor. In Packingtown there were thousands of tons of fertilizer in a building, heaped here and there.

It was to this building that Jurgis came daily. For a month his secret prayers were granted, but early in

June there were men wanted in the fertilizer mill. The boss beckoned to him, and in ten minutes Jurgis had gone to work. Here was one more difficulty for him to conquer!

Before him was one of the vents of the mill in which the fertilizer was being ground—rushing forth in a great brown river. Jurgis's task was to shovel the fertilizer into cars. He could not see six feet in front of him, and in five minutes he was a mass of fertilizer. In 15 minutes he had a headache and was almost dazed. Still he fought on, and a half-hour later he began to vomit.

At the end of that day of horror, he could hardly stand. He had a sense of humor and later used to think it fun to board a streetcar and see what happened. Now, however, he was too ill to notice how the people in the car began to gasp. In a minute the crowded car was nearly empty. At home he smelled so that he made all the food at the table taste like fertilizer, and set the family to vomiting. And still Jurgis stuck it out! At the end of the week he was a fertilizer man for life.

So passed another summer. They were again able to pay their debts and begin to save a little. It was too bad the boys should have to sell papers. They were learning to swear, to pick up cigar stumps and smoke them. Worse, the boys were getting out of the habit of coming home at night. Jurgis declared they would return to school in the fall, and Elzbieta would work, her place at home taken by her 13-year-old daughter Kotrina.

Elzbieta got a job at a sausage machine. She had to stand motionless all day. For the first few days it seemed to her she could not stand it. She was working in a dark hole. There were always puddles of water on the floor and a sickening odor.

Provided you did not look at the people, the machines were perhaps the most wonderful things in the entire plant. On one side of the room men shoveled in loads of meat and wheelbarrows of spices; the whirling knives ground the meat fine and added potato flour and water. Then one of the women would take a casing, put the end over a nozzle, and press a lever, and a stream of sausage meat would shoot out. Visitors would then notice the tense set face of the woman and realize it was time to go. The woman did not go; she stayed right there, hour after hour, day after day. She was apt to have a family to keep alive, and ruthless economic[20] laws had arranged that she could only do so by keeping this job.

Chapter 14

With a member trimming beef in a cannery, and another working in a sausage factory, the family had a firsthand knowledge of Packingtown swindles. It was the custom to either can spoiled meat or chop it up into sausage. Jonas had once told them of the miracles of chemistry that could give to any sort of meat any color and flavor and odor. They could now study the whole of the spoiled-meat industry from the inside. They read new meaning into that Packingtown joke— that they used everything of the pig except the squeal.

The packers had a pickle that destroyed the odor of spoiled hams. And yet, in spite of this, some of the hams had an odor so bad that a man could hardly

---

20. economic of or related to matters of money

bear to be in a room with them. For these, the packers had a second and much stronger pickle that destroyed the odor.

It was only when the whole ham could not be saved that it came into the department of Elzbieta. There was not the least attention given to what was cut up for sausage. There would come all the way back from Europe sausage that had been rejected and was moldy and white. It would be doused and made over again into sausage. Meat would be stored in great piles in rooms, leaky water would drip over it, and rats would race around on it. The packers would put out poison, and then poison and rats would go into the hoppers together. There were things that went into the sausage that made a poisoned rat seem a tidbit.

Such was the work Elzbieta did. It was brutalizing work. It left her no time to think, no strength for anything. She was part of the machine she tended. Little by little, she fell silent. She would meet Jurgis and Ona in the evening, and they would walk home. Ona, too, was falling into the habit of silence. Ona, who had once gone about singing like a bird, was sick and miserable, and barely had enough strength to drag herself home. Then they would eat, and because there was only misery to talk of, crawl into bed, and get up again, and go back to the machines.

Yet the soul of none of them was dead, only sleeping, and now and then would waken. These were cruel times. They were beaten; they had lost the game. They had dreamed of freedom, of a chance to be decent and clean and see their child grow up to be strong. And now it was all gone. Six years more of toil they had to face before the end of payments on the house; and how certain it was that they could not stand another six years of such a life! Ona learned to weep silently—her mood and Jurgis's so seldom came together now!

Jurgis had troubles of his own. He would never speak of it, but battling this demon took all the manhood he had. Jurgis had discovered drink. He was working in the steaming pit of hell, day after day, week after week, until there was not a part of his body that did its work without pain. From the unending horror there was a deliverance—he could drink! He could forget the pain and be master of his thoughts, of his will. His dead self would stir in him, and he would find himself laughing with his companions. He could be a man again.

With the first drink, he could persuade himself that he could eat a meal, and that was fine. With the second drink, he could eat another meal, but there would come a time when he could eat no more. Then to pay for a drink was unthinkable extravagance. One day, though, he drank up all that he had in his pockets. He was happier than he had been in a year. He knew the happiness would not last, though, and was savage with those who would wreck it; and then he was sick with shame. Afterward, when he saw the despair of his family, and added up the money he had spent, tears came to his eyes.

It was a battle that had no end, that never could have one, but Jurgis did not realize that clearly. He simply knew he was always fighting. The time came when nearly all his conscious life consisted of a struggle with the craving for liquor. He would have ugly moods when he hated Ona and the family because they stood in his way. He was a fool to have married. It was all because he was married that he was forced to stay in the yards.

The few single men in the fertilizer mill had something to think about while they worked—the memory of the last time they had been drunk. As for Jurgis, he was expected to bring home every penny. He was supposed to eat his dinner on a pile of fertilizer dust.

That was not always his mood, of course. He still loved his family. But just now was a time of trial. Poor little Antanas was down with the measles, and there was no one to attend to him but Elzbieta's young daughter Kotrina. At night Antanas was tied down so he would not kick the covers off him. He would lie and scream for hours. He was burning with fever and his eyes were running sores.

Yet this was not as cruel as it sounds, for Antanas was quite able to bear his sufferings. He was the child of his parents' youth and joy. In general, he toddled around the kitchen with a lean and hungry look; he always wanted more to eat.

It seemed he had taken all his mother's strength. Ona was with child again, and it was dreadful to contemplate. Even Jurgis understood that yet other agonies were on the way.

Ona was going to pieces. She had developed a cough like the one that had killed old Dede Antanas. She would have frightful headaches and fits of weeping. Jurgis would go half mad with fright, becoming half hysterical himself. Ona would pull herself into his arms and beg him to stop, that she would be better. So she would lie and sob out her grief while he gazed at her as helpless as a wounded animal.

Chapter 15

The winter was coming, more menacing and cruel than ever. A day before Thanksgiving came a snowstorm. By evening two inches had fallen. Jurgis tried to wait for the women, and went into a saloon to get warm. He had two drinks and then ran home to escape the demon of drink. He fell asleep, and found the next morning that Ona had not come home. There was a foot of snow on the ground.

Jurgis set off at a run for the yards, stopping to inquire along the way. He found out that Ona had checked out from work the night before. After that there was nothing to do but wait. Fifteen minutes after work began at seven, Ona emerged from the snow mist. She staggered forward and fell into his arms.

"What has been the matter?" he cried, anxiously. "Where have you been?"

"I couldn't get home," she exclaimed. "I had to go home with a friend." Jurgis drew a deep breath and noticed she was sobbing. "I tried to get home, but I was so tired! Oh, Jurgis, Jurgis!"

He was so glad to get her back that he did not think of anything else. He let her cry, and then left her at the packinghouse door, with her ghastly white face.

Three days from Christmas, Ona did not come home again. Something more serious must be wrong this time, Marija said. Jurgis listened crossly. She must have gone home with her friend, he said, and was snoring before the two had closed the door.

In the morning, however, he was up an hour before the usual time and went to the friend's house. "Where's Ona?" he demanded.

"She isn't here," Ona's friend replied. "What made you think she would be?"

"I thought she would be here the same as before," Jurgis said.

"Ona has never spent the night here," the friend answered, quickly. "She must have meant somewhere else."

There was nothing more to be said, and he excused himself and went away. He walked on half dazed. She had deceived him! What could it mean? He went to Ona's work. All morning he stayed there, with no thought to his own job. At noon he went to the police. Finally, he set out for home. On the way, he suddenly stopped short. Ona was on a streetcar. He tore after the car. She got out, and he followed her home, suspicious, his mind in a turmoil.

Elzbieta met him at the door. "Ona is asleep," she whispered. "She's been very ill. She was lost on the street all night. She came in after you left this morning."

"You are lying to me," Jurgis said, his teeth set. He pushed her aside and strode to the bedroom door. Ona was sitting on the bed and turned a startled look on him as he entered.

"Where have you been?" he demanded.

Her face was white as paper and drawn with pain. She began speaking low and swiftly. "I—I think I have been out of my mind. I walked all night, I think—"

"You are lying to me," said Jurgis, fiercely. "What are you doing that you have to lie to me? You told me you had been to your friend's house, and you hadn't. Where were you?"

It was as if he struck a knife into her. She seemed to go all to pieces, staring at him with horror in her eyes, and tottered forward, stretching out her arms to him.

But he stepped aside and let her fall. She caught

herself and sank down, bursting into frantic weeping. She was sobbing and choking, and then her voice would begin to rise into screams. "Jurgis! Jurgis!" she said. "Believe that I know best—that I love you! And do not ask me—it wasn't my fault—it is nothing. You do not really need to know. We can love each other the same!"

"Answer me!" he cried, and smashed his fist upon the table. "Tell me where you were last night!"

She began to whisper. "In a house downtown—"

"What house? What do you mean?"

"The forelady's house," she gasped.

And suddenly, the horrible truth burst over him, and he staggered. "Tell me! Who took you to that house for prostitues?"

She tried to get away. He thought it was the pain of his clutch—he did not understand that it was the agony of her shame. Still, she answered him, "Connor, the boss—"

"Tell me," he whispered at last. "Tell me about it."

"I did not want—to do it. I only did it—to save us. He told me all of us would lose our jobs. He meant it."

Jurgis's arms were shaking so that he could hardly stand up. "When—when did this begin?" he gasped.

"He—he wanted me. He offered me money. He said he loved me. Then he threatened me, and one day he caught hold of me—he would not let go—he—he—"

"When was this?"

"Two months ago. He wanted me to come—to the house. He said that we would not have to work. He made me come there—in the evenings. I told you— you thought I was at the factory. I didn't want you to know. He was getting tired of me—he would have left me alone soon. I am going to have a baby. And now you will kill him—and we shall die."

Jurgis ran like one possessed to the factory where Ona worked. In an instant more he saw Connor, a big, red-faced man who smelled of liquor. He saw Jurgis and turned white. Jurgis knocked him backward. The next moment Jurgis was on top of him, burying his fingers in his throat, screaming in his fury. In the end, men choked the breath out of Jurgis, and he lay still until they summoned a patrol wagon.

Chapter 16

A barred door clanged upon Jurgis, and he sat down upon a bench and buried his face in his hands. At first he felt dull satisfaction. He had done the scoundrel pretty well. But then, little by little, he began to see that his nearly killing the boss would not help Ona, or help feed her and her child. She would certainly lose her job. It was not for himself he suffered—what did a man who worked in Durham's fertilizer mill care about anything that the world might do to him!

They had only a few dollars now. They had just paid the rent, and it was overdue again. So they would lose the house. Three times now the agent had warned them he would not tolerate another delay. They would lose it all; they would be turned out into the street. Jurgis had all night to think about this, and his mind landed on the worst possibilities.

In the morning, he had another ride in the patrol wagon. He was taken to a large, white-walled room. In front sat a stout person. Our friend realized vaguely he was about to be tried. He wondered what for—whether his victim might be dead and, if so, what they would do with him. Jurgis sat gazing about the room in hopes that one of the family would come, but in this he was disappointed. Finally, he was led before the judge, and a lawyer for the company appeared before him. Connor was under a doctor's care. Jurgis was held in jail, for he did not have the money to get out on bail.

Then they took him to the county jail, nine or ten miles from the stockyards. They left him his money, 15 cents. Jurgis was required to stay in the bath longer than any of the others in the vain hope of getting the smell out of him.

The cells were in tiers. There was no window. Some had books to read and cards to play, but Jurgis was left alone in darkness and silence. He could not sleep; the same thoughts lashed him like whips.

In the distance there was a church-tower bell that rang the hours. Then, suddenly, the bells were ringing music. The meaning broke over him—this was Christmas Eve! He had forgotten it entirely! A whirl of new memories and grief rushed into his mind. In far-off Lithuania they had celebrated Christmas, and even in Packingtown they had not forgotten it. Last Christmas Day Jurgis and Ona had toiled, but still they had found strength to take the children for a walk to see the store windows all decorated and ablaze with Christmas lights.

Great sobs shook Jurgis. The family would spend Christmas in misery and despair, with him in prison and Ona ill and their home in desolation. Why must they ring Christmas bells! His wife might be dying, his baby starving—and they were ringing Christmas chimes! They put him in a place where the snow could not beat in; they brought him food and drink. Could they find no better way to punish him than to leave three weak women and five helpless children to starve?

Their justice—it was a lie, it was a hideous lie. It was only force. They had murdered his old father, broken and wrecked his wife, crushed his whole family. Now they were through with him—and because he had gotten in their way, this was what they had done to him!

These midnight hours were the beginning of his rebellion, of his unbelief. He had no wit to say that "the system" was crushing him to earth; that it was the packers, his masters, who had bought up the law of the land. He only knew that he had been wronged, and that the world had wronged him. Every hour his soul grew blacker, and he dreamed new dreams of vengeance, of raging hate.

Chapter 17

In the morning, a jail keeper opened the door and let in another prisoner. He was a dapper young fellow with a light brown mustache and a graceful figure.

"Well, pal," he said, "good morning."

"Good morning," said Jurgis.

The newcomer inspected the mattress. "Looks as if it hadn't been slept in."

"I didn't want to sleep last night," said Jurgis.

"There's a devil of a stink in here," the man said suddenly. "What is it?"

"It's me," said Jurgis. "Fertilizer. I work in the stockyards—at least I did until the other day. It's in my clothes."

"What are you in for?"

"I hit my boss."

"I see. You're an honest workingman?"

"What are you?" asked Jurgis.

"I?" The other laughed. "I crack safes."

"Oh," said Jurgis. "You mean you break into them?"

"Yes," laughed the other, "that's what they say." He spoke like a man of education, a gentleman. "What's your name? I'm Jack Duane." He seated himself and soon put Jurgis on a friendly footing. He drew Jurgis out, and heard about his life. Then he told stories about his life.

Jurgis could not help but be interested in the talk of Duane—the first educated man to whom he had ever spoken. The young fellow had an amused contempt for Jurgis as a working mule; he, too, had felt injustice, but instead of bearing it, he had struck back hard.

He was a college-educated man who had been robbed of an invention by a great company. Jurgis asked him what had led to safecracking. A man he had met, Duane replied. Jurgis was so clearly who he pretended to be that his cell mate was open with him. It was pleasant to tell of adventures in crime when Jurgis was so full of admiration.

Duane introduced him to many of the other prisoners. All life had turned to rottenness in them. They were thieves of pennies and dimes, trapped by thieves of millions of dollars. Jurgis tried not to listen. They frightened him with their savage mockery. He spent a week in their company, with no word of home. He paid for a postcard with one of his 15 cents. His companion wrote a note to his family, telling where he was and when he was to be tried. There came no answer. The day before New Year's Jurgis bade good-bye to Jack Duane, who gave Jurgis his address, and made him promise to look him up.

Jurgis rode in the patrol wagon back to court for trial. One of the first things he made out was Elzbieta and her daughter, Kotrina, looking pale and frightened. He stood gazing at them in helpless agony. He brooded over this, and suddenly a man came in—Connor!

He never took his eyes off his enemy. The fellow was still alive, which was a disappointment, in one way. Connor took the witness chair and told his story. The wife had been discharged for disrespect to him, he claimed, and then he had been almost choked to death.

"You admit attacking him?" asked the judge of Jurgis.

"I hit him, sir," said Jurgis.

"What have you to say for yourself?"

Jurgis hesitated. He had learned to speak some English, so he tried once or twice, stammering, to the annoyance of the judge, who was gasping at the odor of fertilizer. Finally a translator stepped up. Jurgis explained how the boss had taken advantage of his wife and threatened her with the loss of her job. The judge interrupted with, "Well, why didn't she complain?"

Jurgis began to explain that they were very poor—

"I see," said the judge, "so you thought you would knock him down. Is there any truth to this, Mr. Connor?"

"Not a particle. They tell some such tale every time you have to discharge a woman—"

"I know," said the judge. "Thirty days and costs."

It was only when the policeman started to lead him away that Jurgis realized sentence had been passed. "Thirty days!" he cried. "What will my family do? I have a wife and baby—they will starve!"

"You should have thought of that before you committed the assault," said the judge dryly.

Jurgis saw Elzbieta staring in fright, and then they led him away. This time he was taken to the "Bridewell," a jail even filthier and more crowded than the last. There the prisoners worked breaking stone.

One day there was a visitor to see him. Jurgis turned white, and so weak at the knees he could hardly move. Little Stanislovas was in the visitors' room. At the sight of someone from home Jurgis nearly went to pieces.

"Well?" he said, weakly.

"They—they sent me to tell you that Ona is very sick, and we are almost starving. We can't get along. We thought you might be able to help us."

Jurgis gripped the chair tighter, and his hands shook. "I—can't—help you," he said.

"Ona cries all the time. A man came for the rent and said he would turn us out of the house. And Marija—she's cut her hand, and she can't work, and we can't pay the rent and we have no coal and nothing to eat and the man at the store—it's so cold all the time. Last Sunday it snowed, a deep snow, and I couldn't get to work."

"You little villain!" Jurgis cried. "You didn't try!"

"I did!" said Stanislovas, shrinking in terror. "The third day Ona went with me, but she had lost her place. The forelady wouldn't take her back."

Jurgis could not speak.

"Ona's been trying to get other work, but she's so weak. And my boss would not take me back, either—Ona says he knows Connor. They've all got a grudge against us now. I've got to sell papers with the boys and Kotrina—she does best because she's a girl. Mother hasn't any work because the sausage department is shut down. She begs at houses, and people give her food, only she didn't get much yesterday."

Little Stanislovas went on, and Jurgis stood, saying not a word but feeling that his head would burst.

Little Stanislovas stopped. "You cannot help us?"

Jurgis shook his head.

"When are you getting out?"

"Three weeks yet," Jurgis answered.

"Then I might as well go," the boy said, uncertain.

Jurgis nodded. Then, remembering, he put his hand into his pocket and drew out the fourteen cents. "Here. Take this to them."

Stanislovas took it, and after a little more hesitation, started for the door. "Good-by, Jurgis," he said, and walked unsteadily out of sight.

For a minute or so Jurgis stood clinging to his chair, swaying. The keeper touched Jurgis on the arm, and he turned and went back to breaking stone.

Chapter 18

Jurgis did not get out as soon as he expected. To his sentence were added "court costs," but nobody had told him this. Finally a keeper came with the word that his time was up at last, so he put on his old fertilizer clothing and heard the prison door clang behind him.

He stood on the steps, bewildered. He could hardly believe that the sky was above him and he was free. Jurgis had had enough to eat in the jail, but fear had worn him thin. He began walking, forgetting everything in the fever of his thoughts. He was coming to the rescue! He was free! He could do battle against the world!

He passed endless blocks of two-story shanties and saloons, and came at last to the stockyards. He jumped a streetcar and was soon home. But what was wrong with the house? It was a different color! The broken window was fixed and curtains were in the windows!

The door opened and a big, rosy-cheeked youngster came out. "What are you doing here?" Jurgis gasped.

"I live here!" said the boy, angrily.

"You live here! Then where's my family?"

"Hey, ma!" called the boy. "Here's a fellow says he owns this house."

"What's that?" a stout Irishwoman demanded.

"Where is my family?" he cried wildly. "This is my home! What are you doing in my home?"

"You must be mistaken," the woman said. "This is a new house. They told us so. I bought the house three days ago, and they told me it was all new," she said. She made him understand at last that she knew nothing. Then suddenly he thought of the Lithuanian woman on the next block. She would know! He turned and started at a run. The woman came to the door. Yes, yes, she told him. The family had moved; they had not been able to pay the rent and had been turned out into the snow. The house had been repainted and sold the next week. The family had gone back to the boardinghouse where they had stayed when they first came to the yards.

Jurgis turned and staggered away. He sat down and hid his face in his hands and shook with dry, racking sobs. Their home! They had lost it! Grief, despair, rage overcame him. The whole agony came back. The 300 dollars they had scraped together, their toil month after month for the 12 dollars, the interest, the repairs. Dede Antanas had died to earn that money.

Jurgis could see the truth now. That first lying advertisement, the slippery agent, the trap of the extra payments. And then all the tricks of the packers—the shutdowns, the lowering of wages! The mercilessness of the city, of the country in which they lived, of its laws that they did not understand! And they could do nothing.

The boardinghouse was a good two miles away, and when he saw the dingy house his heart was beating fast. He ran up the steps and began to hammer on the door. The old woman gave a start when she saw him.

"Is Ona here?" he cried breathlessly.

"Yes," was the answer, "she's here." From inside the house came a wild, horrible scream. The voice was Ona's. For a moment Jurgis stood paralyzed with fright. Then he ran past the old woman. He stared at the women in the kitchen, and then came another piercing scream.

It was from the rear of the house and upstairs. Jurgis bounded for the stairs, and heard a voice behind him.

"No, no, Jurgis! Stop!" It was Marija.

"What do you mean?" he gasped.

"You mustn't go up," she cried.

Jurgis was half-crazed with fright. "What's the matter?" he shouted. "What is it?"

Marija clung to him. He could hear Ona sobbing above. "Jurgis, you mustn't go up! It's the new child!"

"The new one! But it isn't time," he added, wildly.

Marija nodded. "I know. But it's come."

Then again came Ona's scream, and he heard her sobbing, "Let me die! Let me die!"

Marija dragged him into the kitchen. Again Ona cried out. "Go away, Jurgis," Marija said. "It's all right—"

"Who's with her?" Jurgis demanded.

"She's—all right. She's with Elzbieta," Marija said.

"But the doctor!" he panted. "Someone who knows!"

"We have no money," Marija whispered.

Above her voice Jurgis heard Ona again. There was no arguing with him. Why, she was being torn to pieces! Had they tried to get a doctor? They might pay afterward, they could promise—

Marija told him how she tried to find a midwife, but they had demanded 25 dollars, and they still owed for two weeks' rent. It looked like Jurgis was going to collapse. Suddenly the old woman who owned the boardinghouse hobbled toward him. "Take this," she said, handing him some coins. The other women emptied their pocketbooks. Jurgis took the money, thrust it into his pocket, and started away at a run.

Chapter 19

Jurgis saw a midwife's sign. "My wife!" he said to the fat woman inside frying pork and onions. "Come quickly!"

"I have not had my dinner," she said, "but if it is bad—what will you pay?"

Jurgis showed her the coins. The woman laughed.

"I have nothing more," he said in desperation. "I would pay, but I haven't got it! *I haven't got it!*"

"Wait. I go." At the house, the midwife gave a cry of dismay. "What sort of place is this for a woman to have a child? You should be ashamed!"

Then Marija and the other women pushed Jurgis out of the house. "Go away! You are only in the way."

So Jurgis went outside, where the rain had turned to snow. He remembered a saloon nearby where he used to eat his dinner. They might have mercy on him there.

Jurgis went straight to the bar. "I've been in jail, and I've not had a thing to eat, and my wife's ill," he said to the saloon keeper.

The saloon keeper gazed at his haggard face and pushed over the bottle. "Fill her up!" he said. Jurgis drank and ate. His soaked clothes began to steam, and the stench of fertilizer filled the room. Men would not come into a place that smelt of Jurgis. The saloon keeper finally said, "Say, I'm afraid you'll have to quit."

He was used to the sight of human wrecks, but Jurgis still had reminders of decency about him. "Come this way," he told Jurgis, and led him to the cellar stairs. So Jurgis spent the night. At four in the morning he left.

The women were still huddled about the stove. "Not yet," Marija said, shaking her head slowly. The midwife came down, her arms smeared with blood.

"I have done my best," she said. "I can do nothing more—there is no use to try."

The midwife looked around, and saw Jurgis, and shook her finger at him. "You pay me the same. It's not my fault if I can't save the baby."

Marija, seeing the beads of sweat on Jurgis's forehead, broke out in a low voice, "How is she?"

"She fights hard, that girl—she is not quite dead."

And Jurgis gave a frantic scream. "*Dead!*"

"She will die, of course," said the other, angrily. "Her baby is dead now."

Jurgis rushed up the ladder. In a corner was a bundle of rags and old blankets. Ona was so shrunken that he would scarcely have known her, and white as

chalk. He staggered toward her with anguish.
"Ona! Ona!"

She did not stir. He caught her hand in his. "Look at me! It is Jurgis come back—don't you hear me?" There was the faintest quivering of her eyelids, and her eyes opened—one instant. There was a flash of recognition between them, and he stretched out his arms to her. But it was all in vain. She faded from him and was gone. He clutched her hands, pressed her to him, but she lay cold and still. She was dead! His cries of despair echoed through the house. He was stumbling through the shadows, groping after the soul that had fled.

She was only a girl, she was barely 18! Her life had barely begun. He turned to Kotrina, who had just come in from selling papers. "Have you any money?"

"Nearly three dollars," she said, frightened.

"Give it to me," he said and headed for a saloon.

Chapter 20

But a big man cannot stay drunk long on three dollars. The next day Jurgis came home, sober and sick, realizing he had spent every cent the family owned.

Ona was not yet buried, but the police had been notified. On the morrow they would take Ona's body to potter's field.[21] Elzbieta was out begging pennies now to pay for a mass for her, and the children were starving to death while he had been spending their money on drink. So spoke the woman who owned the boardinghouse, scornfully.

---

21. **potter's field**   a public burial place for the poor

It was dark in the attic. They could not afford any light. It was also about as cold as outdoors. In a corner sat Marija holding little Antanas. Jurgis crept like a whipped dog and sat by the body. He shed no tears, being ashamed to make a sound. He never dreamed how much he loved Ona until now that she was gone. His old love, which had been beaten to death, awoke. He saw her in Lithuania, beautiful as the flowers, singing like a bird. He saw her with her tenderness, her heart filled with wonder. The long cruel battle with misery and hunger had hardened him, but it had not changed her. Every angry word he had spoken came back to him and cut him like a knife.

Elzbieta came back, having begged the money for a mass and gotten a bit of stale rye bread for the children to eat. She said not a word of reproach to Jurgis. Already Elzbieta had choked down her tears, grief crowded out of her soul by fear. She had to bury her stepchild, but she had done it before and each time had risen up to do battle for the rest.

Elzbieta pled with Jurgis. Ona was dead, but the others must be saved. There was Antanas, his own son. Ona had given Antanas to him—he must treasure him and protect him. It was terrible that they were not able to bury Ona properly, but so it was. Their fate was pressing, and they had not a cent. So Elzbieta went on. She was wild with dread at the thought that Jurgis might leave the family as Jonas had.

With Ona's dead body beneath his eyes, Jurgis could not abandon his child. Yes, he said, he would get to work at once, without even waiting for Ona to be buried. They might trust him. He would keep his word.

And so he went out the next morning, heading for the fertilizer mills, to see if could get back his job.

But the boss shook his head. "There is nothing for you here."

"Didn't I do my work?" Jurgis asked.

"There will be nothing for you here, I said."

Jurgis knew saloon keepers who would trust him for a drink and a sandwich, and members of his old union who would lend him a dime. It was not a question of life or death for him. Meanwhile, Elzbieta was begging and the children would bring home enough to keep them alive. At the end of the week, Jurgis stumbled on a chance. "Worked in the yard before?" the man asked.

"At Brown's killing beds and the fertilizer mill."

"Why'd you leave there?"

"The first time an accident, and then jail."

"Well, I'll give you a trial. Come tomorrow."

Jurgis rushed home with the wild tidings. The remnants of the family had quite a celebration. Jurgis was there a half-hour before opening the next day.

"Oh," said the foreman. "I promised you a job, didn't I? Well, I'm sorry. I can't use you." There was the same hostile stare that he had had from the boss of the fertilizer mill, and he knew there was no use.

At the saloons the men told him about the meaning of it. Poor devil, he was blacklisted.[22] Knocked down his boss? He had as much chance of getting a job in Packingtown as being mayor of Chicago. They had him on a list. He could never work for the packers again.

For two weeks more Jurgis went looking for a job. Once he loaded a truck for half a day. Another time, he carried an old woman's suitcase for a quarter. In the end Jurgis got a chance through an old friend from his union days. The friend worked in one of the giant factories of the Harvester Trust, and told

---

22. blacklisted   to be put on a list of people who are disapproved of or avoided

Jurgis he would speak to the boss. Jurgis trudged five miles, and passed through a waiting crowd of people. After the foreman looked him over, he told him he could have a job.

Jurgis found that the harvester factory was the sort of place reformers pointed to with pride. Its workplaces were roomy, and there was a restaurant where workers could buy good food at cost. This new place came to seem a kind of heaven to Jurgis.

It was an enormous factory, covering 160 acres and employing 5,000 people. Each one of the hundreds of parts of a machine were made separately. Where Jurgis worked, there was a harvesting machine that stamped out the iron plates; another mashed them into shape. They were piled into a truck, and it was Jurgis's job to wheel them to the room where the machines were assembled. This was child's play for him, and he got $1.75 a day for it. With this he paid the 75 cents a week the attic in the boardinghouse cost. He got back his overcoat, which Elzbieta had pawned when he was in jail.

Jurgis began to pick up heart again and make plans. When Marija was well they could start over and save. At work was a man, a Lithuanian, who went to school at night to learn English and served as a watchman on the weekends. That was the sort of thing Jurgis had dreamed of two or three years ago. He might do it still. They might move into this neighborhood and he would really have a chance. With a hope like that, there was some use to living. He laughed to himself as he thought how he would hang on to this job!

Then one afternoon, his ninth of work in the place, he saw a group of men crowded before a sign on the door. When he went over they told him that tomorrow his department of the harvester works would be closed until further notice!

Chapter 21

There was not half an hour's notice—the works were closed! It had happened before, said the men. They had made all the harvesting machines the world needed, and now they had to wait till some wore out! Thousands of workers were turned out in the dead of winter to join the tens of thousands already homeless. Jurgis walked home heartbroken, overwhelmed. What help were kind employers if they could not stop him from losing his job?

For two days he stayed in the attic and sulked. But then their money was going again, and little Antanas was hungry, and the midwife was after him for money. So he went out once more. For another ten days he roamed the streets, begging for any work. There were a hundred men for every job. At night he crept into doorways. Often, he had to fight, sometimes for a place near the factory gates, now and then with street gangs. At last, on a Sunday, he went home and found that they had been waiting for him for three days— there was the chance of a job for him.

It was quite a story. One of the children was near crazy with hunger these days. He had found a dump where children raked for food, and gorged himself. He came home with a story of how a fine lady had wanted to know about him, and had asked where he lived. She told him she would come to see him.

The lady really came, the very next morning, and climbed the ladder and turned pale at the sight of the bloodstains on the floor where Ona had died. Elzbieta was glad to have someone to listen to all their woes. As she listened the pretty lady's eyes filled with tears. The lady sent a basket of things to eat, and left a letter Jurgis was to take to a man who was boss of a steelworks in South Chicago. "He will get Jurgis a job," she said, smiling through her tears. "If he doesn't, he'll never marry me."

The steelworks were 15 miles away. Jurgis arrived before daybreak. Far and wide the sky was flaring with the red glare that leaped from rows of towering chimneys. A hundred men were waiting where they took new men on. Soon, whistles began to blow, and thousands of men poured like a river through the gate.

Jurgis presented his precious letter. It was two hours before he was summoned. He had never worked in a steel mill before, but he was ready for anything. So they began a tour among sights that made Jurgis stare amazed. The air shook with deafening thunder, and whistles shrieked warnings. Sizzling, white-hot masses of metal sped past him, and explosions of fire and flaming sparks scorched his face. The men worked with fierce intensity, never lifting their eyes from their tasks.

He was taken to a furnace the size of a theater. Jurgis saw three giant caldrons full of something blinding white, roaring as if volcanoes were blowing through it. He saw a caldron tip to the side, and a pillar of white flame poured out, a living fire. At the place where ingots[23] of steel were shaped into long, thin, red snakes, Jurgis got his chance. The rails had

---

23. ingots bars or blocks of metal

to be moved by men with crowbars, and they could use another man. Jurgis took off his coat and set to work on the spot.

It took him two hours to get to work every day, and the trip would cost $1.20 a week. As paying for that was out of the question, he took his bedding and found a lodging house where he could stay for ten cents a night. Every Saturday night he went home and took the greater part of his money to the family. Elzbieta was sorry for this arrangement. She feared he would get in the habit of living without them, and once a week was not often for him to see his baby, but there was no other way.

In a week Jurgis learned to take the miracles and terrors for granted, to work without hearing the rumbling and crashing. From blind fear he went to being reckless and indifferent, like the rest of the men. It was wonderful when one came to think of it, that these men took the interest in the work they did. They had no share in it—they were paid by the hour, and paid no more for being interested. They knew that if they were hurt they would be flung aside and forgotten—and still they would use dangerous shortcuts. One morning as Jurgis was passing, a furnace blew out, spraying two men with liquid fire. Jurgis rushed to help them and lost a good part of his skin from the inside of one of his hands. The company doctor bandaged it up; he got no thanks from anyone and was laid up for eight days without pay.

Antanas was now a year and a half old. He learned so fast that every week when Jurgis came home it seemed he had a new child. The little fellow was Jurgis's one delight. He was terrible to manage, but his father did not mind that. The more of a fighter he was, the better.

It was now April, and the snow had given way to cold rains. The unpaved street in front of their boardinghouse had turned into a canal. Jurgis would have to wade through it to get home, and he could easily get stuck up to his waist in the mire. But he did not mind this much—it was a promise that summer was coming.

Marija had gotten a job as a beef-trimmer, and Jurgis told himself that he had learned his lesson, and there would be no more accidents. At last there was the prospect of an end to their long agony. They could save money again and have a comfortable place. The children would be off the streets and at school again. So once more Jurgis began to make plans and dream dreams.

One Saturday night he jumped off the car and started home. He had 66 hours rest before him and a chance to see his family. When he came to the house, he saw the kitchen crowded. It reminded him of the time he had come home from jail and found Ona dying. His heart stood still. "What's the matter?" he cried. A dead silence had fallen in the room, and he saw that everyone was staring at him. "What's the matter?" he exclaimed again.

Then, from the attic, he heard Marija wailing. He started for the ladder, and the landlady seized him by the arm. "No, no!" she cried. "Don't go up there!"

"What is it?" he shouted.

The old woman answered him weakly. "It's little Antanas. He's dead. He was drowned in the street!"

Chapter 22

Jurgis took the news in a peculiar way. He turned deathly pale, and for half a minute stood in the middle the room, clenching his hands tightly. Then he strode into the next room and climbed the ladder. In the corner was a blanket with a form beneath it; beside it lay Elzbieta.

"How did it happen?" he asked.

"He fell off the sidewalk!" she wailed. The sidewalk was a platform about five feet above the level of the sunken street. "He went out to play. We couldn't make him stay in. He must have got caught in the mud!"

Jurgis stood a few seconds, wavering. He did not shed a tear. He took one more glance at the blanket with the form beneath it, and climbed down the ladder. He went straight to the door and started down the street. When his wife had died, Jurgis made for the nearest saloon. He did not do that now, though he had his week's wages in his pocket. He walked, seeing nothing. Now and then he would whisper to himself: "Dead! *Dead!*"

He went on until dark, and was stopped by a railroad crossing. A long train of freight cars was thundering by. He stood and watched, and an impulse seized him. As the train slowed, he sprang forward and swung onto one of the cars.

When the train started up again, he gripped his hands and set his teeth. There would be no more tears and no more tenderness. He had had enough! This was no world for women and children, and the sooner they got out the better for them. He was now going to think of himself against the world that had tortured him.

The train thundered on. Every mile Jurgis got from Packingtown was another load from his mind. When the cars stopped a warm breeze blew, laden with the perfume of honeysuckle and clover. He sniffed it, and it made his heart beat wildly. He was in the country again! He had been a countryman all his life, and for three long years had not seen a country sight. Now he stared at each new sight—a herd of cows, a meadow full of daisies.

He came to a farmhouse. "I would like to buy some food," he said to the farmer there.

"Ask the woman," said the farmer, nodding over his shoulder. For a dime Jurgis got two thick sandwiches and a piece of pie and two apples. In a few minutes he came to a stream where he lay for hours. There was a deep pool below him, and a wonderful idea rushed upon him. He might have a bath! It would be the first time he had been all the way into the water since he left Lithuania!

The water was warm, and he splashed around like a boy. Afterward he sat down in the water and scrubbed every inch of himself with sand. Then he washed his clothes, piece by piece; as the dirt and grease went floating off downstream he grunted with satisfaction.

After another long sleep, he set off. Before long, he came to a big farmhouse. "Please, sir," he asked the farmer washing his hands at the kitchen door, "can I have something to eat? I can pay." To which the farmer responded, "We don't feed tramps here. Get out!"

Jurgis went without a word, but he saw a field in which the farmer had set out some young peach trees, and as he walked he jerked up a row of them by the roots. That was his answer, and it showed his mood.

The man who hit him would get all that he gave, every time.

Jurgis came to another road, and another farmhouse. He asked here for shelter as well as food, adding, "I'll be glad to sleep in the barn. How much will it cost me?"

"I reckon about twenty cents for dinner. I won't charge you for the barn," replied the farmer. After dinner they sat on the steps and smoked, and the farmer asked, "Why don't you stay here and work for me?"

"I'm not looking for work right now," Jurgis said.

"I'll pay ye good," said the other. "Help's scarce."

"Winter as well as summer?" Jurgis asked quickly.

"No," said the farmer. "Not after November."

"I see," said the other. "That's what I thought. Do you turn out your horses into the snow?" (Jurgis was beginning to think for himself nowadays.)

"It ain't quite the same," the farmer answered, seeing the point. "There ought to be work that a strong fellow like you could get in the wintertime."

"That's what all the fellows think," Jurgis said, "and so they crowd into the cities. When they have to beg to live, people ask them why they don't go into the country, where help is scarce." Then Jurgis bade the farmer farewell.

Such was the beginning of his life as a tramp. He learned to prefer sleeping in the fields. Before long came raspberries, to help him save his money; there were apples in the orchards and potatoes in the ground. When these failed he would use his money carefully, but without worry—he could earn money when he chose.

But Jurgis was not staying. He was a free man now. Think of what it meant to a man whose whole life had consisted of doing a certain thing all day—to now be his own master, facing a new adventure every hour! His health came back to him, the joy and power he had forgotten. He would waken not knowing what to do with his energy, stretching his arms, singing old songs of home. Now and then, of course, he would think of little Antanas, or he would dream of Ona, and stretch his arms to her, and wet the ground with his tears. But in the morning he would get up and stride away.

The men who lived as he lived taught him their tricks: when to beg or steal, and when to do both. Most of the tramps had been workingmen, but had found it was a losing fight, and given up. In July, Jurgis came upon harvest work in Missouri. All over the land there was a cry for labor. They paid them well—the best men could get three dollars a day. Jurgis worked two weeks from dawn to dusk, and ended with a sum that would have been a fortune in the old days. But what could he do with it? Jurgis knew nothing of banking. If he carried it he would be robbed, so all there was to do was enjoy it while he could. He went to the saloons and in the morning he had not a cent. He was sick and disgusted, but he crushed his feelings in his new way.

One night he was caught in a thunderstorm, and sought shelter in a house outside of a town. It was a workingman's house, and the owner was a Slav[24] like himself. He made him welcome. The wife was cooking supper, and he and the man exchanged thoughts.

The woman proceeded to undress her youngest baby to give him a bath. He was about a year old, and a sturdy little fellow. When she put him into the basin he grinned, and spoke in the quaintest of baby accents—and every word of it brought back to Jurgis his own dead little one, and stabbed him like a knife.

---

24. **Slav**   a person who speaks a Slavic language, such as Lithuanian, as his native language

He could bear it no more, in the end, and the memory caused him to burst into tears. Between the shame and the woe Jurgis could not stand it, and rushed into the rain. He finally came to a woods, where he hid and wept as if his heart would break. What despair—to know Ona and his child were gone from him forever!

Chapter 23

Early in the fall Jurgis set out for Chicago again. He traveled on the trains with others, hiding in freight cars. He had 15 dollars, hidden in one of his shoes. When he reached the city he left the others, for he had money and they did not, and he intended to save himself in this fight. He would eat at free lunches—five cents a meal, no more—so he might keep alive two months or more, and in that time surely find a job. He would have to bid farewell to cleanliness, of course, for he would come out of his first night's lodging with his clothes alive with vermin.

He found his places at the steel mill and the harvester works filled long ago. He was careful to stay away from the stockyards. He was a single man now, he told himself, and meant to stay one, to have his wages for his own.

In the end it was through a newspaper that he got a job, after nearly a month. He stood in line, and an hour later told the man he was willing to do anything. A half-hour later he was at work, far underneath the streets of the city, digging tunnels for telephone wires. It was a new tunnel, and so Jurgis knew he had an all-winter job.

He got himself a tenement room for a dollar a week, and got his meals for four more. This left him four dollars extra a week, an unthinkable sum for him. He bought heavy boots and a flannel shirt, and decided not to buy an overcoat. This was an unfortunate decision, for it drove him more quickly into the saloons. He had his corner in an unheated room, and the streets with winter gales. Besides this he had only the saloons—and, of course, he had to drink to stay in them.

Such was his life during the six weeks he toiled underground. Then one night, a car dashed around a corner, striking him and knocking him senseless. When he opened his eyes, he was in an ambulance. They took him to a county hospital, where a surgeon set his arm. Jurgis spent Christmas in this hospital, and it was the pleasantest he had had in America. His only complaint was that they fed him tinned meat, which no man who ever worked in Packingtown would feed his dog. Jurgis used to wonder who ate the canned corn beef. Now he knew it was eaten by soldiers and prisoners and inmates.

Jurgis left the hospital after two weeks. That he was utterly helpless concerned no one. He might have sued the company, but he did not know this. As he must certainly would not be able to work for a couple of months, his landlady decided she would not keep him on trust.

So Jurgis went out on the streets. It was bitterly cold, and snow was falling. He had no overcoat and no place to go. He had $2.65 in his pocket, with no way of earning more. Words could not paint the terror that came over him as he realized this.

In the beginning he thought only of getting out of the awful cold. He went into a saloon and bought a drink, which afforded him the privilege of loafing; the fact that Jurgis was an old customer entitled him to a somewhat longer stop. Then he went to another place, where he could not resist the hot beef stew. When he was told to move on, he made his way to another place, where the bartender gave him a tip—there was a religious revival meeting on the next block, where hundreds of hoboes would go for shelter.

By eight o'clock the place was crowded. There were hymns and a speech. Terror kept Jurgis awake—he knew he snored badly, and to have been put out would have been terrible. Jurgis listened and found his soul filled with hatred. What did this preacher know about suffering, with his body warm and his belly full! They were part of the order that was crushing men! They had food and clothing, and so they might preach to hungry men, and the hungry men must be humble and listen!

At eleven the desolate audience filed out into the snow. This was in January, 1904, and the country was on the verge of "hard times." The police stationhouse would open its doors, but before that door men tore each other like savage beasts. Jurgis, with his broken arm, did not get in. There was no choice then but to spend another dime at a boardinghouse. It broke his heart to do this after he had wasted his night at the meeting and on the street.

That was one day, and the cold spell lasted for fourteen. After six days Jurgis's money was gone, and then he went on the streets to beg for his life. He would approach every likely looking person, telling his woeful story. When he got a dime or a nickel he would dart back to a saloon, and his victim, seeing him do this, would vow never to give to a beggar again. The victim never paused to ask where else Jurgis might have gone.

Poor Jurgis might have been expected to make a successful beggar. He was sick, and had no overcoat, and shivered pitifully. But alas, he was a blundering amateur. He was pale and shivering, but the professionals were made up with cosmetics, and had studied the art of chattering their teeth. There were professional beggars who had thousands in the bank. Some had padded stumps in their sleeves. The less fortunate had maimed themselves or burned themselves. Every day the police would drag hundreds off the streets, and in the detention hospital you might see them, with hideous, beastly faces, bloated with disease, barking like dogs, raving in delirium.

Chapter 24

One day Jurgis experienced the one big adventure of his life. It was late, and he had failed to get money for lodging. He was begging among the theater crowds, and when he saw a man coming, he placed himself in his path.

"Please, sir," he began, and gave his story. The man did not interrupt, and Jurgis came to a breathless stop.

"Whazzat you say?" the man asked, in a thick voice. "Poor old chap! Been up against it, hey?" He put his hand on Jurgis's shoulder. He was about 18, and handsome. He wore a silk hat and an expensive overcoat. "I'm hard up, too, my good friend. Whazzamatter?"

"I've got a broken arm—" Jurgis began.

"You'll get over that," the boy said. "Whuzzit you want me to do?"

"I'm hungry and I haven't any home," Jurgis said.

"No home! Stranger in the city! Better come home with Freddie Jones. We'll have some supper."

They began to walk. Jurgis was trying to think what to do. He knew he could not pass any crowded place with his new acquaintance without being stopped.

"Is it very far?" Jurgis inquired.

"Not very," replied the other. "Tired, are you? We'll call a cab! You call, and I'll pay. How's that?" And he pulled out a roll of bills. It was more money than Jurgis had ever seen in his life.

"Looks like a lot, hey?" said Master Freddie. "Fool you, ole chappie—they're all little ones! I'll be busted in one week more, sure thing. That's one more reason why I'm going home. 'Hanging on the verge of starvation,' I says to my father—'Send me some bread.' I'll run away if he don't."

The young gentleman rambled on—and Jurgis trembled with excitement. He might grab that roll of bills and be out of sight before the other could collect his wits. But Jurgis had never committed a crime in his life, and now he hesitated too long. Freddie got one bill loose and stuffed the others back into his pocket.

"Here, old man," he said, "You take it." By the light of a window Jurgis saw that it was a 100 dollar bill! "Pay the cabbie and keep the change."

A cab was driving by. Jurgis called, and it sprang to the curb. Freddie climbed in with difficulty, Jurgis following, when the driver shouted "Get out, you!"

Jurgis was half obeying, but his companion said to the cabbie, "Hey, whazzamatter with you, hey?"

The carriage started and the boy fell asleep. Jurgis

debated if he should try to get the bills, but he was afraid to go through his companion's pockets. He had the hundred, and would have to be content with that. When the cab stopped, Master Freddie sat up with a start. Before them loomed an enormous granite mansion. Jurgis thought the young fellow must have made a mistake. It was impossible that a person could have a home like a hotel. But he followed in silence.

They rang the bell and the door opened. A butler stood holding it, gazing silent as a statue. Then Jurgis felt his companion pulling and he stepped in. Jurgis's heart was beating wildly. He could see a vast hall and a great staircase. The floor was made of marble. From the walls, paintings loomed like sunset glimmers in a shadowy forest. The man at the door had moved toward them. He helped Freddie with his coat and hat. They went down the great hall, and into the dining room. The butler pressed a button, and lights flooded the room. Jurgis looked at the domed ceiling and an enormous painting, and thought he was in a dream palace. On a table black as ebony gleamed wrought silver and gold.

"Ever seen anything like it before, hey, ole chappie?"

"No," said Jurgis.

"Come from the country, maybe?"

"Yes," said Jurgis.

"Aha! I thought so. Lossa folks from the country never saw such a place. Old man Jones's place—Jones the packer—Beef Trust man. Made it all out of hogs, too, old scoundrel. Ever hear of Jones the packer?"

Jurgis managed to stammer out, "I have worked for him in the yards."

"What!" cried Master Freddie. "*You*! In the yards! Why, say, thass good. Why Hamilton, let me introduce you—old friend. Works in the yards." The

stately butler bowed his head but made not a sound. "Hamilton, we'll have a cold spread and some fizz."

They went up the great staircase. The butler opened a door before them, and they staggered into a study. Beyond, a door opened onto a bedroom, and beyond that was a swimming pool of the purest marble.

The butler had closed the study door, and he stood by it, watching Jurgis every second. Then in came a man with a folding table and behind him two men with covered trays. They first spread the table and then set out the contents of the tray. There were slices of meat, tiny sandwiches, peaches and cream (in January), little fancy cakes, and half a dozen bottles of ice-cold wine.

Freddie seated himself at the table; the waiter pulled a cork, and Freddie poured three glasses down his throat. He gave a long sigh, and, perceiving that the attendants embarrassed Jurgis, said to them, "You may go."

Freddie turned to the table. "Eat!" he cried. "Pile in!" So Jurgis began, without further talk. When he got started his wolf-hunger got the best of him, and he did not stop until he had cleared every plate. "Gee whiz!" said the other, who had been watching in wonder.

Then he held up the bottle. "Lessee you drink now," he said, and Jurgis took the bottle and turned it up to his mouth, and a wonderful liquid ecstasy poured down his throat. "Good stuff, hey?" said Freddie, sympathetically.

The cheerful youngster rattled on and then closed his eyes, sleeping. For some minutes Jurgis sat reveling in the strange sensation of the champagne. Then the butler came in, and pointed to the door. "Get out of here!" he whispered, scowling. Jurgis surrendered and started for the door. At the front door the butler snarled, "Hold up your hands!" Jurgis took a step back. Understanding the butler meant to search him, he answered, "I'll see you in hell first!"

"Do you want to go to jail?" demanded the butler, menacingly. "I'll have the police—"

"Have' em!" roared Jurgis. "But you won't put your hands on me till you do! I haven't touched anything in your damned house, and I'll not have you touch me!"

So the butler, who was terrified that his young master should waken, stepped suddenly to the door, and opened it. "Get out of here!" he said, and then gave him a ferocious kick that sent him down the great stone steps, and landed him sprawling in the snow at the bottom.

Chapter 25

Jurgis got up, wild with rage, but the door was shut. In spite of the last humiliation, his heart was thumping. Yet he was in a difficult situation. He had not a single cent but that 100 dollar bill, and he had to change it! To get it changed in a lodging would be to take his life in his hands. He would certainly be robbed before morning. The only other thing he could think of was a saloon. Finding one where the bartender was alone, he went in.

"Can you change a 100 dollar bill?" he asked.

"Lemme see it," the bartender said. Jurgis approached him warily, and finally handed it over.

"Humph," the bartender said, gazing at the ragged, ill-smelling tramp. "Want to buy anything?"

"Yes," said Jurgis. "I'll take a glass of beer."

"All right," said the bartender. "I'll change it." He took the bill and poured a glass of beer. Then he counted out two dimes, a quarter, and 50 cents. "Here." Jurgis waited. "My 99 dollars," he said. "What 99 dollars?" said the bartender. "My change!" Jurgis cried. "From my 100!" "Go on," said the bartender. "You're nutty!" Jurgis stared at him with wild eyes. Then he hurled the glass at his head. The bartender shouted, "Help! Help!" A policeman came in, a club descended, and Jurgis dropped like a log. The bartender went behind the bar and stowed the 100 dollar bill in a safe place.

In a few minutes Jurgis was in a cell. In the morning at court the bartender told his story. The prisoner had come in, drunk, with a dollar bill. He had been given change, demanded 99 dollars, and attacked him.

"Your honor," said Jurgis when he told his side, "I gave him a 100 dollar bill to change, and he wouldn't give me the change."

"You gave him a 100 dollar bill?" asked the judge. "Where did you get it?"

"A man gave it to me," Jurgis said. "I had been begging." There was a titter in the courtroom.

After hearing how Jurgis had something to drink— something that burned—the judge said, "I guess that will do. You ought to stop drinking if you can't control yourself. Ten days and costs. Next case." Poor Jurgis could not know that the owner of the saloon paid five dollars each week to the policemen and that the bartender was a henchman of the Democratic leader of the district.

Jurgis was driven back to Bridewell for a second time, and encountered—Jack Duane! The young fellow was so glad to see Jurgis he almost hugged him. "Why, if it isn't the Stinker!" he cried.

Jurgis told his story. Most didn't believe it, but Duane knew Jurgis could never have made up that yarn. "Why don't you come with me when you get out, Jurgis?" he said. And so, when he was turned out of prison, Jurgis went straight to Jack Duane. He went with gratitude, for Duane was a gentleman with a profession. Jurgis did not understand that a man who could be trusted was as rare among criminals as among any group.

Duane spend the day laying bare the criminal world of the city and showing Jurgis how to make a living in it. That night, they went out. When a man passed, Duane stole out, and Jurgis heard a thud and a cry. Jurgis came out to hold him, and Duane went through his pockets. They divided the spoils, and Jurgis got 55 dollars. That was a good haul, the other said, better than average.

In the morning, Jurgis was sent out for a paper; one of the pleasures of crime was reading about it. Learning how the victim would lose three fingers because he was half-frozen when he was found worried Jurgis. "He never did us any harm," Jurgis said, reflectively.

"He was doing it to somebody as hard as he could, you can be sure of that," said his friend.

Jurgis got a glimpse of the high-class criminal world from Duane. He learned how millions bought elections, how the police and fire departments had license to swindle. The law forbade prostitution and gambling, so that brought in the madams and the poolroom men. The seller of diseased meat, and the owner of falling-down tenements, and the fake doctor—all banded together in a league with the politicians and the police.

A month ago Jurgis had nearly starved on the streets; now he had entered a world where all the good things of life came freely. Before long Jurgis learned the meaning of "pull" and why Connor had been able to send him to jail. One night Jurgis got drunk, and quarreled, and ended up in a jail cell. He sent for one of his friends, who explained to the judge that Jurgis was a decent fellow who had been indiscreet. So Jurgis had his fine suspended.

There were ups and downs in the business, but there was always a living. Early in April were the city elections, and that meant prosperity for all. Jurgis met with men from both parties, and heard about a number of ways to make himself useful, including buying votes.

About this time Jurgis saw again the man named Harper who had signed him up to become an American citizen. A couple of days later Harper said he could get Jurgis a job in Packingtown if he did as he was told, and kept his mouth shut. Harper was a right-hand man of Scully, the Democratic boss of the stockyards.

Jurgis, who had no known politics, was to work at the stockyards and help elect a Republican as alderman.[25] Scully agreed that he would elect the Republican. In return, the Republicans would agree to put up no candidate the year after that, when Scully was running for the other position of alderman. The Democrat running was a rich man whom Scully was willing to sacrifice.

The reason Scully was willing to pay Jurgis to help the Republican was because a new threat was on the horizon. The Socialists were rising. Marija's friend, the musician Tamoszius, was a Socialist, and had tried to interest Jurgis, but Jurgis had never quite got it straight. But Harper explained that the Socialists

---

25. alderman a member of the legislative body in a town or city government

were the enemies of America's institutions. Socialists could not be bought. Scully was afraid that if the Democrats did not vote for the Republican choice, they would choose the Socialist over the rich capitalist[26] Democrat. Jurgis's job was to talk up the good points of the Republican, and the bad points of the Democrat, and to give out beer.

When he had heard all this, Jurgis demanded: "But how can I get a job in Packingtown? I am blacklisted."

Harper laughed. "I'll attend to that," he said.

So Jurgis went to the stockyards again and met Scully. It was Scully who was to blame for the unpaved street where Jurgis's child had drowned, and Scully whose company sold him the house, and then robbed him of it. But Jurgis knew none of these things. To him, Scully was a mighty power, the most important man he had ever met.

Scully gave him a letter for a manager at Durham's, who read it. "What do you wish to do?" he asked.

"Anything, sir," said Jurgis—"only I had a broken arm, so I have to be careful."

"Would it suit you to trim hogs?"

"Yes, sir," said Jurgis. And so Jurgis marched into the hog-killing room, a place where, in days gone by, he had begged for a job. Now he smiled at the frown on the boss's face when he was told to put Jurgis on. It would crowd his department, but he said only, "All right."

And so Jurgis became a workingman again, sought out his old friends, joined the union, and began to root for the Republican. Jurgis distributed notices, and brought out the crowds, and gave out beer. On election morning he was out at four o'clock, voting half a dozen times himself, and some of his friends as often. He had 100 dollars to spend for votes, and three

---

26. capitalist   one who believes in a system where private individuals or companies own business

times he came for another 100, and kept not more than 25 of each. At the end there was joy over the triumph of popular government over a rich man.

Chapter

After the elections Jurgis kept his job in Packingtown. It was an easy job, and habit kept him at it. Besides, Mike Scully had told him that something new might "turn up" before long. He had nearly 300 dollars in the bank.

He had found out at the boardinghouse that Elzbieta and her family had gone downtown, and so he gave no further thought to them. He went with a new set now, young unmarried fellows. He would go to the cheap music halls with them, or to petty gambling parlors.

In the spring, the yards were full of talk of a strike. The price of dressed meat had gone up nearly 50 percent, and the cost of beef on the hoof had gone down. The union was pressing for an increase to 18 cents an hour for unskilled men, but the packers were unwilling. A million and a half men in the country were looking for work, a 100,000 right in Chicago. The union decided to strike. The next day, 60,000 men walked off and the "Beef Strike" was on.

Jurgis walked over to see Mike Scully, who lived in a fine house. Scully looked nervous and worried. "What do you want?" he demanded when he saw Jurgis.

"I came to see if you could get me a place during the strike," the other replied. In that morning's paper, Jurgis had read about a fierce attack on the packers by Scully.

Therefore, Jurgis was not a little taken aback when Scully said, "Why don't you stick by your job?"

Jurgis started. "Work as a scab?"[27] he cried.

"What's that to you? The packers will treat a man right who stands by them," Scully said.

"But how could I ever be of use to you in politics?" asked Jurgis.

"You couldn't anyhow," said Scully abruptly. "Hell, man! You're a Republican! Do you think I'm always going to elect Republicans? The strike will be over in a few days—the men will be beaten; and meantime what you can get out of it will belong to you. Do you see?"

Jurgis saw. He went to the yards, where the foreman was directing the feeble efforts of clerks and office boys. "I have come back," Jurgis said. The boss's face lit up.

"Good man!" he cried. "Come ahead!"

"I think I should get a little more wages," said Jurgis.

"Of course," replied the other. "What do you want?"

Jurgis's nerve almost failed him, but he clenched his hands. "I think I ought to have three dollars a day."

"All right," the boss said. Jurgis could have kicked himself when he learned the clerks were getting five dollars! Jurgis was provided with a cot and three meals a day. The police and the strikers wanted no violence, but another party did want violence—the press.

On the first day Jurgis and three men went outside to get a drink. They went through the gate. A picket jerked off the hat of one of them with a cry of "Scab!" and a dozen people came running. Jurgis and the others fled into the yards. Two hours later, Jurgis saw

---

27. scab a person who works while others are on strike

armfuls of newspapers with the headline: "VIOLENCE IN THE YARDS!" The story was all over the country the next day.

The next morning Jurgis was sent to one of the superintendents, who asked him about his experience. Jurgis was told he was to become a boss in the killing department. The packers had been left most in the lurch there, precisely the place where they could least afford it. Fresh meat must be had, or public opinion would change.

An opportunity such as this would not come twice, and Jurgis seized it. But if he took the job, would they turn him out after the strike? The boss said he might trust Durham's—they proposed to teach these unions a lesson.

Our friend flung himself at his task. It was a weird sight on the killing beds—clerks fainting from the heat and the stench. Many of them did not want to work and often had to rest. As there was no system, it might be hours before their boss discovered them.

Jurgis, flying here and there, did his best to organize such a force as this. He had never given an order in his life, but he had taken enough of them. Soon he roared and stomped like the bosses of old. There was no bringing order out of this chaos, though. If a man forgot to come back, there was nothing to be gained by seeking him, for all the rest would quit. This custom of resting meant a man might work at more than one place and earn more than one five dollars a day. When Jurgis caught a man at this he fired him in a quiet corner, but with a ten dollar-bill to Jurgis he soon had his job back.

But in spite of their best efforts to recruit workers, the packers were discouraged. About 90 percent of the men had walked out, and with the price of meat up 30 percent, the public was clamoring for a settlement. They made an offer to submit the issue to arbitration,[28] and within ten days the union accepted the offer. The strike was settled. The union men were to be reemployed.

That night the word went out to hire no union leaders. The next morning the superintendent came out and chose man after man that pleased him, but no men who were union stewards. The men were wild with rage. "We all go back or none of us do!" cried a hundred voices. Within a half-hour the strike was on again.

The stockyards were now the camping place of 20,000. Each day the packers added new workers, and Jurgis was one of their agents. He had gotten used to being a master of men. Because of the heat and the stench, and because he was a scab and despised himself, he raged at his men and drove them to exhaustion.

One night when he was on his way back to his bed, he turned into a room and saw Connor, the man who had seduced his wife, sent him to prison, ruined his life! When Jurgis saw him, rage boiled in him, and he flung himself at the man and pounded his head on the stones.

So Jurgis spent the night in the stockyards' station house. He sent word of his plight to Harper, Scully's man. "Connor!" Harper cried. "Not Phil Connor! They talked of sending him to the legislature! There's nothing I can do—unless there's this. I could have your bail reduced, and you could pay it and skip."

"I have 300 dollars," Jurgis said.

"I'll try to get you off for that," Harper said. "I'd

---

28. **arbitration**   the hearing of a case by a person chosen by both sides

hate to see you go to prison for a year or two." Harper reduced the bail. Jurgis, overwhelmed with gratitude, took the $3.39 left and got off a streetcar at the end of Chicago.

Chapter 27

So Jurgis was a tramp once more. He now had higher standards, and he desired all sorts of things. But never had his chances of getting a job been worse. There were a million people out of work, and Jurgis could not go anywhere people knew he was "wanted."

At the end of ten days Jurgis had only a few pennies. Raw terror possessed him. He passed a warehouse, and a boss offered him a job, and then laid him off because he was not strong. It was all he could do to keep from breaking down and crying like a baby.

He stole a cabbage, and found out about a free soup kitchen. All these horrors afflicted Jurgis because he was always contrasting them with what he had lost. One night he heard a band, and knew it was a political meeting, and that meant shelter. He found himself in a hall, and the sight almost brought tears to his eyes, thinking of when he, too, had been among the elect. He knew if he fell asleep he would snore loudly, but the seat was so comfortable he did fall asleep, and snored. Jurgis was thrown out and found himself in the rain.

He got into the shelter of a doorway. He must begin begging. Coming down the street was a lady. "Please, ma'am," he said, "can you lend me the price of a night's lodging?" Then he stopped short. It was a woman who had come to his wedding. She was as surprised as he.

"Jurgis! What is the matter with you?" she gasped.

"I've had hard luck," he stammered. "I have no home."

"I don't have my purse with me," she said, "but I can do something better—I can tell you where Marija is."

At the mere mention of Marija, his being cried out with joy. She would help him. He took the address and soon found himself in front of a large brownstone. He asked for Marija and was let in.

Then, however, came another knock, and men rushed in. "Police! Police!" yelled the girl at the door. The girls made fun of the police. One of them, in a red kimono, screamed, drowning out all other sounds. Jurgis gave a start, and said, "Marija!"

"Jurgis!" she said in amazement. "How did you know I was here?" He told her about running into their old friend on the street. He knew now he was in a place where men paid for women's company. He had seen a great deal of the world, and yet it gave him a painful start that Marija should do this. They had always been decent people. But then he laughed. Who was he, pretending to decency!

"How long have you been living here?"

"Nearly a year. I had to live and I couldn't see the children starve. I got sick, and Stanislovas died—"

"Dead! But how did he die?"

"Rats killed him. He fell asleep in a factory where he was working, and got locked up, and rats killed him."

Jurgis sat, frozen with horror. "Are the rest alive?"

"Yes. They live not far from here. They're all right. I take care of them. I'm making plenty of money now."

"Do they know you live here—how you live—as a prostitute?"

"Elzbieta does, and maybe the children do now. It's nothing to be ashamed of—we can't help it."

"Perhaps you think I did you a dirty trick, running away as I did, Marija—"

"No," she said, "I don't blame you. We never have. You did your best. The job was too much for us. If I'd known what I know now, we'd have won out."

Jurgis was sunk in grief and memories; his old hopes and yearnings came flooding in. Thoughts of the sufferings of his family had become strangers to his soul. Now these were beckoning to him, but soon they would die—and so the last spark of manhood in his soul would flicker out.

Chapter 28

The men were let go the next day. Jurgis walked home with Marija. Jurgis noticed there were rings under her eyes. "Have you been sick?" he asked.

She was silent a moment. "It's morphine," she said. "I seem to take more of it every day. The madam gives the girls dope when they first come. I've got the habit."

"How long are you going to stay?"

"Always, I guess. What else could I do?" Then came a girl with the message that the madam wanted Marija.

Jurgis got up, and she gave him the new address of the family. "You go there. They'll be happy to see you."

So Jurgis went out and thought it over. He decided he would first try to get work, but got none. Then he saw there was another meeting at the hall where the political speech had been, and he decided to go in and sit down and rest. Almost every seat was filled. Jurgis went back to his thoughts. In the end his head sank forward and again he fell asleep.

Suddenly there was a woman's sweet voice in his ear. "Try to listen, comrade;[29] you may be interested." Jurgis was startled. Comrade! Who had called him comrade? The woman who had spoken was young and beautiful, and wore fine clothes, and a look of excitement on her face. What was going on, to affect anyone like that? It must be what the man was saying. So it occurred to Jurgis to turn and listen to the speaker.

The speaker was tall and gaunt, his voice vibrant with pain and longing. Suddenly it seemed to Jurgis as if the speaker had singled him out. He was saying, "You return to your daily round of toil, to be ground up for profits in the worldwide mill of economic might! And each day the struggle becomes fiercer. I speak with the voice of the millions who are voiceless! For the little child who staggers with exhaustion, for the man who lies sick, leaving his loved ones to perish!

"In the crowd tonight there will be some one man who is desperate. And to him my words will come like a sudden flash of lightning. He will leap up with a cry and stride forth a free man at last.

"Tonight there are 10,000 women shut up in foul pens, driven by hunger to sell their bodies. There are a million people, men and women and children, who toil every hour they can see for enough to keep them alive. There are a 1,000 who are the masters of these slaves. They riot in luxury. The whole of society is in their grip. They own not merely the labor of society; they have bought the government. Is there a man so hardened that he dare say it will continue forever?

"Can you not see that the task at hand is your task? The voice of the poor, demanding that poverty shall cease! The voice of power, wrought out of suffering! He

---

29. **comrade** a fellow member of a group

lifts himself, and the bands are shattered, he rises—
towering, gigantic; he springs to his feet—"

The audience came to its feet with a yell, and Jurgis
was with them, shouting. He felt himself a mere man
no longer—there were powers within him undreamed
of. The words of this man were to Jurgis like the
crashing of thunder in his soul. Jurgis had ceased to
hope and to struggle—he had come to terms with
despair, and now the hideous fact was made plain to
him! He stood there, his clenched hands upraised,
roaring in the voice of a wild beast. When he could
shout no more, he stood there gasping, whispering
hoarsely to himself, "By God! By God! By God!"

Chapter 29

Jurgis realized the speech was over. He sat with his
hands clasped, trembling in every nerve. He had never
been so stirred in his life. He could not think; he was
stunned. A new man had been born. He was free! Even
if he were to suffer, nothing would be the same; he
would understand it. He would have something for
which to fight.

The chairman of the meeting came forward and
spoke. His voice sounded thin. He said the speaker
would now take questions. Why should anyone want to
ask questions! The thing was not to talk, but to get
hold of others and rouse them, to organize them for
the fight! When the meeting broke up, Jurgis was in
agony. He would go out, and he would never be able to
find this again! Desperation seized him. He must find
the speaker.

He pushed in a stage door. The speaker sat with his shoulders sunk and his eyes half closed, his face ghastly pale. A big man stood near him, saying, "Stand back a little, please; can't you see the comrade is worn out?"

Jurgis stood watching. Now and then the man would look up, and once, his glance rested on Jurgis. An impulse seized Jurgis. "I wanted to thank you, sir!" he began in breathless haste. "I couldn't go away without telling you—I didn't know anything about it all—"

The big man was back. "The comrade is too tired—"

"Wait," the other said, holding up his hand. "You want to know more about socialism?"

"Is it socialism? I didn't know. I want to help. I have been through all that."

"Where do you live?" asked the other.

"I have no home," said Jurgis. "I am out of work."

"You are a foreigner, are you not?"

"Lithuanian, sir."

The man thought for a moment. "Where is Ostrinski? Would you see if he has gone yet?"

Ostrinski was a little man, wrinkled, very ugly, and slightly lame. But his handclasp was hearty, and he spoke in Lithuanian, which warmed Jurgis to him. "You want to know about socialism? Let us go out and take a stroll, and talk." Ostrinski asked where he lived, and Jurgis had to explain that he had no home. At the other's request he told his story. "You have been through the mill, comrade! We will make a fighter out of you!"

When he understood that Jurgis would have to sleep in a hallway, he offered him his kitchen floor. "Perhaps tomorrow we can do better," he said. "We try not to let a comrade starve."

All over the world, Ostrinski said, the world was forming into two classes. There was the capitalist class, with its huge fortunes, and the rest, bound into slavery by unseen chains. The enslaved workers would be at the mercy of their exploiters until they organized. It was a slow process, but it would go on. In Chicago the movement was growing by leaps and bounds. Nowhere else were the unions so strong, but the strikes generally failed, and as the unions were broken up the men were coming over to the Socialists.

Ostrinski explained the organization of the Socialist party. There were locals in the towns, and in Chicago a publishing house that issued a million and a half Socialist books every year. All this was within the last few years. Jurgis listened to the little man, and he seemed scarcely a less wonderful person than the speaker. He was poor, and yet how much he knew! Jurgis wanted to get to work.

That was always the way, Ostrinski said. When a man found socialism he expected to convert the whole world the first week. After a while he would realize how hard a task it was. Ostrinski would take him to the next meeting and introduce him, and he would join the party. Anyone who could not afford the dues might be excused from paying. The Socialist party was a truly democratic organization—there were no bosses. So far the rule in America had been that one Socialist made another Socialist once every two years; at that rate they would carry the country in the election of 1912.

Jurgis sat lost in wonder. Ostrinski showed him how the Beef Trust crushed all opposition, and was preying on the people. Jurgis remembered how he had watched the hog killing and had come away glad he was not a hog. Now his new friend showed him that a hog was just what he had been. What they wanted from a hog was profits, and what they wanted from the workingman was the same thing. Jurgis would find glimpses of the Beef Trust everywhere, from city government to poultry and fruit and eggs and vegetables. The people were tremendously stirred up over this, but nobody had a remedy. It was the Socialists' task to prepare them for the time when they would seize the machine called the Beef Trust. They would use it to produce food for everyone. It was an hour before Jurgis could get to sleep, for all he could think of was the glory of that vision of the people of Packingtown marching in and taking possession of the stockyards!

Chapter 30

Jurgis had breakfast with Ostrinski and his family, and then went home to Elzbieta. When he went, instead of saying what he had been planning to say, he started telling Elzbieta about the revolution! At first she thought he was out of his mind, but when she was satisfied that he was sane on all subjects but politics, she troubled herself no further. She would even go to a meeting now and then, and plan her next day's dinner amid the storm.

Jurgis continued to look for work. One day he was passing a hotel and decided to go in. He found the owner in the lobby and asked for a job.

"I can do anything, sir," he said.

"Would you be a porter? I've just discharged one who drinks. It's hard work. You'll have to clean floors and fill lamps and handle trunks—"

"I'm willing, sir."

"All right. You can begin now, if you like."

So Jurgis went to work, and paid a visit to Ostrinski to tell him, and discovered that the owner of the hotel was a state organizer of the Socialist party. The next morning Jurgis went to his employer and told him, and the man seized his hand and shook it. "That lets me off the hook! I didn't sleep all night because I had discharged a Socialist!"

The owner was the kindest-hearted man who ever lived, and a passionate Socialist. His hotel was a hotbed of political activity; all the employees were men who belonged to the Socialist party. Every night there was an animated conversation in the lobby. All this radicalism[30] did not hurt the business; the radicals flocked here, and travelers found it amusing.

Of course, the owner of the hotel had soon heard Jurgis's story, and he would say, in the middle of an argument, "Here's a man who's seen every bit of it!" Jurgis would drop his work, and tell the story. When Jurgis would give the formula for "potted ham," or talk about the condemned hogs made into lard, his employer would sit by and encourage him. Then the owner would explain how the Socialists had the only remedy for such evils, and how like the Beef Trust, there were the Oil Trust and the Coal Trust.

Such was Jurgis's new life. To keep the hotel a thing of beauty was his joy in life. His acquaintances at the hotel were men who had come up from the social pit. There was only one difference between the Socialists and the rest: The Socialists were men with hope.

---

30. radicalism   the practice of favoring extreme
     revolutionary change

It was so obvious to Jurgis! You would talk to a poor devil who worked endlessly, who never took a vacation, who had never been able to save a penny. When you started to tell him about socialism, he would sniff and say, "I'm not interested in that—I'm an individualist!"

The agony of such things was almost more than Jurgis could bear, but there was nothing to do but keep at it. For instance, it was quite marvelous to see the difference a year had made in Packingtown—the eyes of the people were being opened! The Socialists were sweeping everything before them with victories that election. Scully and the Democrats were at their wits' end. They brought in a South Carolina senator who denied that the Democratic party was corrupt; it was always the Republicans who bought the votes. Here Jurgis began shouting furiously "It's a lie! It's a lie!" After which he went on to tell them how he knew it—he had bought them himself! He would have told them more, had not a friend shoved him into a seat.

Chapter 31

One of the first things Jurgis had done after he got a job was to go see Marija. "I've got work now, and so you can leave here," he told her.

But Marija only shook her head. There was nothing else for her to do, she said—and besides, she took dope. "I'll never stop. I'll stay here till I die, I guess." That was all she would say. So he left, disappointed and sad.

His outward life was commonplace. He was just a hotel porter, but in the realm of thought, his life was an adventure. One night he was asked to go to a gathering. The invitation was from a millionaire who was not a party member, but was in sympathy with the organization. He would have as his guest that night the editor of a big eastern magazine, who wrote against socialism but did not really know what it was. The editor was interested in the subject of "pure food," however, which Jurgis could speak about.

The house was a little two-story structure, filled with books. Jurgis joined the eight people there, three of them ladies, and was terrified should they expect him to talk.

The conversation ranged over the destiny of civilization, marriage, and religion. After much argument, the company managed to agree to two carefully worded propositions: First, that a Socialist believes in common ownership and democratic management of the means of producing the things needed in life; second, that the way to bring this about was by organizing the wage earners. Each man would be credited with his labor and debited with his purchases, and production and consumption would be automatic. War would be inconceivable, after the triumph of the people. The people did not start wars.

Socialism, too, would mean that meat was eaten less. "As long as we have wage slavery, it matters not how repulsive a task might be," one said. "But as soon as labor is set free, the price of such work will begin to rise. Eventually, people who want to eat meat will have to do their own killing—and how long do you think the custom will survive then?"

Only a few hours after this gathering came election day. The entire country seemed to hold its breath. Jurgis and the rest of the hotel staff could hardly stop to finish their dinner before they hurried off to the big hall the party had hired for the evening. When the final counts were in, the Socialist vote was over 400,000—an increase of almost 350 percent in four years. In Chicago, the vote in the city had been 6,700 in 1900, and now was 47,000. The party leaders were surprised by the tremendous vote that came from the stockyards. In the spring of 1903 the vote had been 500, and in the fall of that year 1,600. Now, one year later, it was over 6,300—and the Democratic vote only 8,800!

At a big hall, a speaker took the platform, and two thousand pairs of eyes were fixed on him. "Organize! Organize!" was his cry. "This election will pass, and the excitement will die, and people will forget about it. It rests with you to find these men who have voted for us, and bring them to our meetings, and organize them and bind them to us!

"Everywhere in the country tonight, the old party politicians are studying this vote, and nowhere will they be more quick or cunning than in our own city. But we have the greatest opportunity that has ever come to socialism in America! We shall organize the workers and marshal them for victory! We shall sweep the opposition before us—and Chicago will be ours! *Chicago will be ours!* CHICAGO WILL BE OURS!"

REVIEWING YOUR READING

CHAPTERS 1–4

FINDING THE MAIN IDEA

1. In the first chapter, the author is mainly telling the reader about
   (A) the first time Jurgis and Ona met. (B) Jurgis's first job.
   (C) Jurgis's and Ona's house. (D) the wedding feast of Ona and Jurgis.

REMEMBERING DETAILS

2. Jonas cries out when he sees the sign "J. Szedvilas" because
   (A) it is a Lithuanian name. (B) it is a boardinghouse, and they need a place to stay. (C) J. Szedvilas is the friend who had made his fortune in America. (D) J. Szedvilas is his brother.

DRAWING CONCLUSIONS

3. The wedding guests probably do not pay their share of the costs because
   (A) they do not have the money. (B) in this new country, the traditions have broken down. (C) they assume that the bride and groom will pay, as in the old country. (D) they do not know it is expected.

IDENTIFYING THE MOOD

4. The mood the author describes in the packinghouses can best be described as
   (A) cheerful. (B) dull. (C) frantic. (D) slow.

CRITICAL THINKING

5. **Comprehension** Why do you think it is important for Ona's and Jurgis's family that the couple have an elaborate wedding feast?

6. **Evalution** Why do you think Upton Sinclair describes the packing yards in so much detail?

7. **Knowledge** Why is the family anxious about buying a house? List reasons to support your answer.

CHAPTERS 5-9

FINDING THE MAIN IDEA

1. This section is mostly about

   (A) the differences between Lithuania and America. (B) the jobs immigrants get in the United States. (C) Jurgis's interest in the union. (D) the family's gradual understanding of the world of Packingtown.

REMEMBERING DETAILS

2. Dede Antanas gets a job by

   (A) proving he can work quickly. (B) promising to join the union. (C) offering to do work that women normally do. (D) paying to get a job.

DRAWING CONCLUSIONS

3. Sinclair probably included the description of Stanislovas's job to show

   (A) how children are exploited. (B) how efficient the machines in the parking plant are. (C) how long Stanislovas has to work each day. (D) how uninteresting the work is.

IDENTIFYING THE MOOD

4. When Marija loses her job and Jurgis is working less and less, the mood is one of

   (A) despair. (B) joy. (C) relief. (D) indifference.

CRITICAL THINKING

5. **Comprehension** Why do you think the family begins to deeply dislike Grandmother Majauszkiene, the neighbor who tells them about the history of their house?

6. **Analysis** Compare Jurgis's view of the packinghouses when he first arrives to how he feels once he and his family begin working.

7. **Evaluation** Describe the character of Marija based on what you have learned in the book so far.

CHAPTERS 10-12

FINDING THE MAIN IDEA

1. Chapter 11 is mostly about

   (A) how hard the winter is for the family. (B) Jurgis being injured and staying home. (C) how poor the family has become.
   (D) Ona having a baby.

REMEMBERING DETAILS

2. Ona does not tell her family how difficult her job is because

   (A) she is afraid of what Jurgis would do. (B) she knows she cannot find a better place. (C) she is hoping to find another job.
   (D) all of the above.

DRAWING CONCLUSIONS

3. Jurgis is bitter when he recovers and goes to look for work because

   (A) he sees now that it is too late in the season to get a job.
   (B) he realizes he should have sued his employers. (C) he knows that he has been worn out by his job and no one will want him.
   (D) he knows that Marija can get a better job than he can.

IDENTIFYING THE MOOD

4. What is Jurgis's mood when he asks about the extra costs he will have for the house?

   (A) grim (B) furious (C) relieved (D) unconcerned

CRITICAL THINKING

5. **Comprehension** Why does Sinclair include information about the Beef Trust?

6. **Analysis** What are the results of the difficult winter on the relationship between Ona and Jurgis?

7. **Application** After his accident, Jurgis cannot find work. What do you think the family will do if Jurgis continues to be unemployed?

CHAPTERS 13-16

FINDING THE MAIN IDEA

1. Chapter 16 is mostly about

   (A) how the family loses its house. (B) Jurgis's thoughts after he attacks Connor. (C) Jurgis's misery over spending Christmas Eve without his family. (D) details of Jurgis's time in jail for attacking Connor.

REMEMBERING DETAILS

2. Jurgis's job at the fertilizer plant is

   (A) to wet down the fertilizer beds. (B) to swing the chutes of fertilizer into railroad cars. (C) to shovel fertilizer into beds. (D) to shovel fertilizer into cars.

DRAWING CONCLUSIONS

3. When Sinclair refers to the Packingtown swindles, what he means is

   (A) overcharging the government for poor meat. (B) the way the workers are cheated by the company. (C) what the public is allowed to see of the inside of the packing plants. (D) selling bad meat with incorrect labels.

IDENTIFYING THE MOOD

4. Which of the following best describes Ona's mood when she tells Jurgis where she has spent the night three days before Christmas?

   (A) enraged (B) terrified (C) defiant (D) uncaring

CRITICAL THINKING

5. **Knowledge** For Jurgis, what is the most painful result of his being imprisoned on Christmas? Use evidence from Chapter 16 to support your answer.

6. **Analysis** What do we learn about Jurgis's character from the events in Chapters 13–16?

7. **Evaluation** Which of the jobs that Jurgis and his family have would you least like to have? Explain why.

CHAPTERS 17-19

FINDING THE MAIN IDEA

1. The most important event that happens in these three chapters is

    (A) the family being without food. (B) Ona dying. (C) Jurgis
    being released from jail. (D) Jurgis meeting Jack Duane.

REMEMBERING DETAILS

2. Bridewell is

    (A) a jail. (B) the judge in Jurgis's case. (C) where Jack Duane
    tells Jurgis to go. (D) the midwife Jurgis finds for Ona.

DRAWING CONCLUSIONS

3. When Stanislovas comes to visit Jurgis in jail, Jurgis yells at
    Stanislovas because

    (A) he knows that Stanislovas had not done all he could for the
    family. (B) he needs to blame someone, and Stanislovas is an easy
    target. (C) he always has had a bad temper. (D) he really want to
    yell at Ona, but she is not there.

IDENTIFYING THE MOOD

4. Which of these best describes Jurgis's mood when he realizes that
    he has been sentenced to 30 more days in jail?

    (A) bewildered (B) frantic (C) uncaring (D) bitter

CRITICAL THINKING

5. **Comprehension** Why do you think the poor women at the
    boardinghouse give Jurgis money to find a midwife?

6. **Analysis** Contrast the way that Jack Duane and Jurgis have dealt
    with the system they find in America.

7. **Comprehension** Why does Sinclair have Ona and Jurgis look at
    each other one more time before she dies?

CHAPTERS 20-25

FINDING THE MAIN IDEA

1. Chapter 22 is mostly about

   (A) how little Antanas died. (B) life in the country versus life in the city. (C) Jurgis's realizing how he has been used by the packers. (D) Jurgis's becoming a hobo as a reaction to the death of his son.

REMEMBERING DETAILS

2. Jurgis is careful to stay away from the stockyards when he returns to Chicago because

   (A) he is ashamed to face his family. (B) he considers himself a single man now and does not want to be responsible for his family. (C) the memories of his dead wife and child are too painful to face. (D) he knows he is still blacklisted.

DRAWING CONCLUSIONS

3. Sinclair includes the adventure of Jurgis spending time with Freddie Brown to show

   (A) that some of the rich have feeling for the poor. (B) that not all of Chicago is as grim as the world of the stockyards. (C) the careless way the rich spend the money they get from the work of the poor. (D) that Jurgis is too noble to steal from the rich.

IDENTIFYING THE MOOD

4. Jurgis's mood when he sees the inside of Jones's mansion is best described as

   (A) anger. (B) wonder. (C) fear. (D) satisfaction.

CRITICAL THINKING

5. **Comprehension** Sinclair writes of the good points of the harvester factory, and then has Jurgis lose his job there. What point do you think Upton Sinclair is trying to make by including this detail?

6. **Knowledge** Explain why Jurgis leaves the rest of his family, knowing they are in desperate trouble, and jumps onto a train out of town at the end of Chapter 22.

7. **Evaluation** Should Jurgis be willing to join Jack Duane's criminal world? Why or why not?

CHAPTERS 26-28

FINDING THE MAIN IDEA

1. Chapter 27 is mostly about

    (A) Jurgis learning what has become of his family. (B) how difficult it is for Jurgis to be a tramp now. (C) how Jurgis comes to find out where Marija is. (D) how Jurgis learned to beg.

REMEMBERING DETAILS

2. Jurgis becomes a tramp again because

    (A) he is tired of life in the city. (B) he has attacked Connor again, and will go to jail if he doesn't leave town. (C) the union is after him because he was a scab. (D) he is disgusted with the deceit among the packers.

DRAWING CONCLUSIONS

3. The Socialist speaker inspires Jurgis so much because

    (A) the speaker is Lithuanian. (B) the speaker has a hypnotic voice, and Jurgis is caught up in the reaction of the crowd. (C) he sees a good way to find a new job. (D) the speaker seems to be talking directly to Jurgis about his life.

IDENTIFYING THE MOOD

4. Jurgis's mood after he has talked to Marija is best described as

    (A) joyful. (B) troubled. (C) fearful. (D) optimistic.

CRITICAL THINKING

5. **Comprehension** On page 92, when Jurgis talks to Mike Scully and returns to his job as a strikebreaker, Sinclair writes that "Jurgis saw." Explain what this expression means.

6. **Evaluation** Why do you think Marija is so willing to forgive Jurgis for running off and leaving the family?

7. **Knowledge** How does Jurgis's mood change from the end of Chapter 27 to the end of Chapter 28? What causes the change?

CHAPTERS 29-31

FINDING THE MAIN IDEA

1. The main thing Jurgis does in Chapter 29 is

   (A) learn more about how the Beef Trust works. (B) learn more about Socialism. (C) find out what Marija is doing now. (D) tell others about Socialism.

REMEMBERING DETAILS

2. After the meeting, Ostrinski takes Jurgis home because

   (A) the Socialist speaker asks him to. (B) he is a fellow Socialist. (C) they want to talk more about Socialism. (D) he realizes Jurgis has nowhere else to sleep.

DRAWING CONCLUSIONS

3. When Jurgis talked to working people about Socialism and they told him they were not interested, Jurgis agonized because

   (A) these workers did know who Jurgis was. (B) these workers were not really listening to him. (C) these people would not join the movement. (D) he was afraid they would report him to the police.

IDENTIFYING THE MOOD

4. Which best describes the mood Sinclair want to establish at the conclusion of the book?

   (A) joyful (B) discouraged (C) fearful (D) optimistic

CRITICAL THINKING

5. **Comprehension** Why does Jurgis's employer at the hotel like to have him tell his stories about the packing plants?

6. **Analysis** Compare and contrast Sinclair's view of the union and the Socialist movement.

7. **Evaluation** Describe the future, as the Socialists see it, after they have taken control of the country.